Campbell County, Tennessee
MARRIAGES
1838-1881

BY

BYRON SISTLER

Nashville, Tennessee.

1984

Originally published:
Nashville, Tennessee
1984

Reprinted:
Janaway Publishing, Inc.
2011

Janaway Publishing, Inc.
732 Kelsey Ct.
Santa Maria, California 93454
(805) 925-1038
www.janawaygenealogy.com

ISBN: 978-1-59641-043-5

Made in the United States of America

INTRODUCTION

Where two dates appear on an entry, the first one is the date license was issued, the second (in parentheses) the date marriage was solemnized. If only one date, either the marriage did not take place or at least there was no return to the courthouse.

We transcribed these marriage records directly from a microfilmed copy of the original county marriage books, so error, where it occurs, will usually be our own responsibility. However, it should be remembered that entries in the books themselves were copied from the licenses by clerks, and it is obvious from examining the pages that many of them were not prepared with great care.

In most cases the original licenses and bonds are not available, having been lost or destroyed.

Byron Sistler
Barbara Sistler
Nashville, Tennessee
November 1984

Abner, John to Mary Jane Clark 8-31-1851
Acres, David to Sarah Stanly 1-15-1841
Acres, James to Emily Cross 3-4-1849
Adams, John C. to Nancy Maze 7-25-1851
Adams, Wm. to L. R. McCall 3-30-1844
Adkins, Alvis to Mary Bryant 11-22-1849 (11-25-1849)
Adkins, Christopher to Elizabeth Martin 2-10-1842
Adkins, David to Nancy Faulkner 3-16-1843
Adkins, Elijah to Catharine Adkins 1-11-1847 (1-17-1847)
Adkins, Elijah to Pelina Jane McCarta 12-10-1840
Adkins, Elish to Hannah Bulloch 2-3-1847
Adkins, James to Margaret Tye 1-28-1839
Adkins, Jeremiah to Volentine Bawl 9-4-1840
Adkins, Jesse to Martha Bird 1-27-18487 (2-28-1847)
Adkins, John F. to Elizabeth Jane Bolton 4-11-1870
Adkins, John F. to Sarah Whiten 12-2-18874
Adkins, John T. to Lucy Duncan 12-31-1859
Adkins, John to Fannie Hutson 6-19-1876
Adkins, Joseph to Eliza Smither 12-25-1842
Adkins, Lewis to Izeally Adkins 2-24-1854 (2-26-1854)
Adkins, Luke to Sarah Woosley 2-11-1838
Adkins, M. L. to Nancy Shootman 2-5-1859 (no return)
Adkins, Millard M. to Julia A. Adkins 12-28-1876 (12-29-1876)
Adkins, Milton to L. C. Day 6-26-1874 (6-27-1874)
Adkins, Milton to Lucida C. Day 6-26-1874 (6-27?-1874)
Adkins, Obediah to E. Shelton 9-26-1839
Adkins, Parmack to Polley Harmon 11-18-1848 (11-26-1848)
Adkins, Peter to Rachel Lay 8-27-1880 (9-9-1880)
Adkins, Powell to Manerva Harman 8-26-1873 (8-28-1873)
Adkins, Prior to Pheroba Hewitt 2-24-1859
Adkins, Richd. to E. E. Adkins 4-15-1854 (4-16-1854)
Adkins, Silas to Cenia Wright 8-6-1843
Adkins, Silas to Elzira Adkins 9-18-1873
Adkins, William C. to Jane Lay 8-22-1871 (8-24-1871)
Adkins, Wm. L. to Frances Henson 3-16-1858 (3-18-1858)
Adkins, Wm. to Mary M. Nance 6-27-1861
Agee, Henry C. to Moss Lamar 5-7-1877 (5-17-1877)
Agee, J. C. to Nancy J. McNeely 11-13-1876 (11-16-1876)
Agee, James H. to Mary Corner 11-15-1848 (no return)
Agee, Jessee to Elizabeth Maddin 11-8-1850 (11-21-1850)
Agee, Wm. to Anna Agee 2-3-1876
Agee, Wm. to Mariah M. Madan 6-15-1843 (6-18-1843)
Aikman, William to Martha A. Graves 11-6-1854
Alber?, George to S. J. Rains ?-13-1877
Albert, J. H. to Tempy J. Wilson 4-7-1873

Albert, Jacob H. to Lucinda Johnson 12-9-1868 (1-2-1869)
Albright, Wm. to Nancy Stout 1-4-1843 (no return)
Alder, A. C. to Lucinda Tow 12-12-1846 (no return)
Alder, W. R. to Timanda Raines 10-22-1878
Alder, Willis D. to Sarah Meadors 10-24-1843 (no return)
Alexander, B. W. S. to Love Maupin 10-31-1853 (10-?-1853)
Alexander, Mitchel to Sarah E. Petree 3-3-1849
Alexander, Samuel to Margaret Petree 8-25-1855 (no return)
Alford, Daniel to Nancy Lea 7-21-1849
Allen, Arch to Nancy Jane Duncan 3-13-1869 (3-25-1869)
Allen, Caswell to Lurany Wilson 11-12-1857
Allen, Felix to Jane Skinner 4-13-1854 (4-20-1854)
Allen, Harrison to M. J. Roach 12-15-1877 (12-16-1877)
Allen, Hiram to Mary Jane Lay 7-23-1868
Allen, John to Nancey Brown 1-13-1839
Allen, Joseph to Lewesey Vowal 8-23-1863
Allen, Joseph to Martha Sharpa 8-14-1846
Allen, William to Louisa J. Warner 1-13-1855
Allen, William to Phebe Barron 4-6-1851
Allen, William to Sarah E. Jones 2-7-1870 (2-9-1870)
Allen, William to Sarah Petry 9-20-1872
Allen, Wm. to Catharine Henderon 5-6-1861
Anderson, Cornelius to Emily Davis 6-11-1842
Anderson, Daniel to Serreldia Roads 3-23-1853
Anderson, Eli F. to July A. Lynch 5-27-1865 (6-8-1865)
Anderson, George to Rana Tacket 3-29-1848 (3-30-1848)
Anderson, John C. to Martha J. Maddin 9-15-1855
Anderson, King D. to Susannah Lamore 7-4-1846 (no return)
Anderson, Phillip to Nancy Tacket 1-17-1850 (no return)
Anderson, Speed to Margret Endle 9-10-1876
Anderson, Thomas to Josephine Rogers 5-10-1875
Anderson, Timothy C. to Kiziah Thompson 2-12-1869 (2-21-1868?)
Anderson, Timothy to Jane Roach 1-17-1850 (no return)
Andrews, W. W. to Sousan Sharp 4-14-1879
Angel, Dennis to Elizabeth King 11-30-1848
Angel, Thomas to Nancey Elswic 2-9-1839
Archer, Enoch to Susanah Boulton 9-9-1843
Archer, Hale to Susan Armelly Walden 8-3-1869
Archer, Hiram to Elander Rutherford 8-14-1879
Archer, James to Jane Perkins 12-9-1869
Archer, Tyree to Emly Bolton 4-6-1878
Arvin, Davis to Frances E. Cain 8-7-1850
Ault, Richard to H. Hatmaker 4-4-1855
Ault, Richard to Mary Massingal 9-9-1880 (9-10-1880)
Ausmus, James J. to Mary L. Burke 7-31-1880 (8-1-1880)

Aycock, J. C. to Mary Jane Hammonds 12-1-1868 (12-2-1868)
Ayres (Heirs), John to Elizabeth Snotherly 11-18-1847
Ayres, Claiborn to Nancy Catherine Broyles 7-14-1872
Ayres, Elilhu to Elizabethe Gayler 3-28-1872
Ayres, Elkanah to Lucinda Campbell 2-9-1851
Ayres, James C. to Nancy Dossett 11-3-1870 (11-10-1870)
Ayres, James M. to Mary J. Owens 9-13-1874
Ayres, James to Patsey Ann Smiddy 12-4-1878 (12-5-1878)
Ayres, John to Martha Dagly 11-18-1849 (no return)
Ayres, Samuel O. to Lucinda H. Marrs 9-13-1851 (9-17-1851)
Ayres, William to Mary Rutherford 8-7-1879
Ayres, Wm. B. to Nancy Jane Douglas 5-12-1872
Ayres, Wm. It to Malinda Bolton 11-2-1872 (11-3-1872)
Ayres, Wm. S. to S. C. Marrs 2-6-1847 (2-13-1847)
Bailey, Franklin to Nancy J. Chapman 2-13-1870 (2-14-1870)
Bailey, James Sr. to Sophia Heninger 2-20-1873 (2-23-1873)
Baily, Casuel to Mary A. Roier 11-7-1876
Baily, John to Polly Sharp 12-7-1847 (no return)
Baily, Wm. to Huldy J. Rogers 12-25-1877
Baily, Wm. to Nancy Chambers 8-20-1845 (no return)
Baines, J. L. to Mary Scheues? 4-5-1879
Baird, Aaron H. to Caroline Bowman 12-24-1874
Baird, Andrew C. to Martha J. Gibson 2-9-1854
Baird, Andrew to Louisa Hix 9-?-1864
Baird, Andrew to Rachael Ryan 7-23-1857
Baird, David to Anna Ray 8-19-1880
Baird, Ewell to Mary A. Alleln 5-23-1879 (5-28-1879)
Baird, Franklin to Nannie Guinn 8-30-1879
Baird, George F. to Pheoba Rose 12-27-1858 (1-6-1859)
Baird, John L. to Catherine Lay 12-26-1872
Baird, John L. to Hannah Walden 12-29-1878
Baird, John S. to Hannah Lay 3-29-1855
Baird, Joseph B. to Hanah Stanfill 12-26-1873 (12-28-1873)
Baird, Joseph to Mary Trammel 4-18-1872
Baird, L. M. to Mary Perkins 9-1-1879 (9-4-1879)
Baird, Leedes to Eliza Jane Lay 3-6-1873
Baird, Lewis to Hanah Baird 11-19-1856
Baird, Lewis to Mary Lay 6-10-1852
Baird, Lewis to Nancy Jane Broyles 2-11-1880
Baird, Samuel C. to Sarah Bowman 12-14-1865
Baird, Silas to Louisa Smith 12-3-1876
Baird, Travis to Deneygreen Trammel 6-13-1870 (6-18-1870)
Baird, Travis to Rachel Lay 8-14-1879 (8-17-1879)
Baird, William to Sally Trammel 5-26-1870
Baird, Wm. to Barbara Hatmaker 12-13-1864 (12-14-1864)

Baird, Zebadee to Mary Rose 2-16-1847 (2-18-1847)
Baird, Zebadee to Maryann Creekmore 3-25-1869
Baker, A. to Sarah Web 3-20-1877 (3-23-1877)
Baker, Benjamin to Sarah Vines 9-9-1841
Baker, Calvin D. to Mary Martha Sharp 7-18-1872
Baker, Davis to Susan Broyles 10-23-1870
Baker, Ewens to Rachael Irvin 4-18-1851 (4-20-1851)
Baker, Ewin to Rachael Irvin 4-18-1851 (no return)
Baker, G. W. to Jane Irvin 5-2-1851
Baker, G. W. to N. J. Wilson 6-16-1879 (6-18-1879)
Baker, James to Delila Lay 3-25-1841
Baker, James to Martha Strader 7-13-1877
Baker, Janus to Nancey Thomas 9-24-1840 (no return)
Baker, Joseph M. to Leah Douglas 10-12-1868
Baker, Michael to Mary Ann Thomas 3-22-1845 (3-23-1845)
Baker, Samuel to Margaret Hatfield 1-15-1846 (1-19-1846)
Baker, W. E. to Emmia Whaley 12-9-1880
Baker, Wm. H. to Ann Wier 6-29-1880 (7-1-1880)
Baley, James to Nancy McNeely 1-1-1855 (1-14-1855)
Baley, John to Sally Wright 1-26-1867 (1-27-1867)
Baley, Thos. to Elizabeth Pierce 6-1-1859
Ball, George W. to Sarah A. Hicks 4-2-1859
Ball, James to Elizabeth McFarland 1-25-1844
Ballard, John to Phoeba Cox 8-9-1865
Ballard, John to Sarah McGraw 2-14-1880 (2-20-1880)
Ballard, R. T. to Hanah Broyles 3-3-1870
Ballard, William W. to Elizabeth Smith 11-18-1839 (11-19-1839)
Bailey, William to Mary L. Miller 3-12-1881
Bandell, Martin to Hety Cathrine Mergan 3-23-1864 (no return)
Bane, Cyrenus to Julyatha Cox (no dates) (with 1848)
Barber, John to Nancy Jones 2-24-1839
Barker, Joel to Elizabeth Johnson 4-7-1860 (4-12-1860)
Barlow, Daniel to Elisabeth Dial 4-25-1864 (4-28-1864)
Barnett, J. T. to N. C. H. Lamare 8-16-1870 (8-21-1870)
Barron, Calvin to M. J. Baird 9-19-1878 (9-26-1878)
Barron, Calvin to Nancey Perkins 2-13-1842
Barron, Marion to Julia Siler 8-13-1876
Barrons, Calvin to Canney Baird 5-31-1838
Barton, A. R. to Jane Harmon 11-22-1870
Bashears, Jacob Isom to Martha Jane Huckeby 1-3-1874 (1-4-1874)
Baulton, Lyn to Ann Case 10-22-1840
Bawhuger, A. to Polly Robinson 8-20-1841 (no return)
Bayley, Doctor to Margaret Davis 3-9-1860 (3-15-1860)
Beaird, William to Nancy Barron 9-19-1838
Beam, Daniel Pinkney to Nancy Cole 9-21-1870

Beams, Fealden to Metilda Richmond 9-13-1838
Beams, Joshua to Julia Elison 7-14-1878
Beams, Samuel to Mary Lawson 9-13-1860
Beams, Wm. to Jarelda Walden 2-28-1845
Beard, David to Martha Jane Adkins 1-2-1845
Beard, Hiram to Ama Hicks 6-15-1865
Beard, Joseph to Delila Walden 12-28-1849 (12-29-1849)
Beard, Joseph to Sally Smitih 7-9-1840
Beard, Lewis to Nancy Lay 9-14-1864 (9-15-1864)
Beard, Samuel to Ann Palina Dale 10-20-1842
Beard, Wm. to Elizabeth Hackler 6-8-1871
Bearid, John L. to Elizabeth Campbell 10-30-1873
Bearid, Pryor P. to Nancy Lawson 9-4-1865 (9-10-1865)
Beaver, James to Sally Ann Bolten 3-2-1873
Beech, Album to Emerone Keeny 11-23-1852 (11-24-1852)
Belteon, James F. to Matailda M. Myers 6-16-1877
Benjy, Samuel S. to Elizabeth Dandy 4-6-1859
Bennet, Hudson to Elizabeth Milton 1-28-1849
Bennet, Joseph to Emley Jones 12-6-1877
Bennett, Amos to Nancy Perkins 11-11-1852
Bennett, Caleb to Elizabeth Peach 3-27-1880
Bennett, George W. to Martha Ann Adkins 12-12-1874 (12-20?-1874)
Bennett, Jno. B. to Polley Bennett 4-30-1876
Bennett, John M. to Rebecca A. Carr 1-23-1874
Bennett, Pleasant to Sarilda Mahan 8-7-1879
Bennett, Thomas to Biddy Reeves 2-6-1879
Berkhart, Daniel to Elizabeth Ann Duke 2-8-1871 (2-12-1871)
Berry, Andrew to Elizabeth Green 10-16-1875 (10-17-1875)
Bibee, J. M. to M. E. Lindsay 6-11-1873
Bibee, John to Martha J. Hollingsworth 3-1859 (3-3-1859)
Biggs, Alen to Catharine Thomas 10-19-1856 (10-23-1856)
Biggs, Allen to Ruth Miller 4-15-1852
Bingham, B. D. to Malinda LeForce 12-14-1863
Bird, Enoch to Ollie Adkins 6-13-1880
Bird, Enoch to Ruth Faulkner 7-21-1850
Bird, John to Nancy Miller 12-25-1849
Bird, Joseph to Tilitha Cook 3-27-1846 (4-2-1846)
Bird, Leander P. to Cynthia Perkins 8-11-1853
Bird, Robert to Nancy Blakely 2-23-1845 (2-13?-1845)
Bird, Robt. to Rachel Douglass 4-13-1845
Bird, William to Sally M. Adkins 6-5-1854 (6-6-1854)
Bird, Wm. to Nancy Richmond 7-16-1859
Birge, John to Catherine Phillips 6-28-1880
Black, Isaac to Nancy Doolan 12-27-1865 (no return)
Black, J. M. to Aney White 10-25-1877

Black, John to Nancy Fouse 1-22-1858 (1-23-1858)
Blackwell, William to Elizabeth Selvage 1-16-1845
Blakely, Curtise to Syntha Bord 11-3-1842 (11-10-1842)
Blakely, Hardin P. to Elizabeth Perkins 12-5-1852
Blakely, Uriah to Mary Jane Bennett 1-26-1879
Blankenship, Wm. to Mary Ann Wilson 11-19-1838
Blevins, Armstrong to Margarett Carson 3-18-1839
Blevins, Hiram to Harriett E. Carroll 2-28-1871 (3-2-1871)
Blevins, Thomas L. to Elizabeth Yancy 11-21-1844 (no return)
Blevins, William to Susasn Peerce 4-11-1842
Boatright, H. W. to Lavina Keeny 2-22-1845 (no return)
Boatright, James H. to Susan Jones 2-3-1848
Bolen, Andrew to Mindy Rains 7-30-1876
Bolin, Anderson to Sarah Powers 2-6-1880
Bolin, John to Catharine Cook 12-29-1853
Bolinger, Pres to Lucinda Bullock 12-18-1875 (12-19-1875)
Bolton, Alvis to Martha Rutherford 9-24-1878 (9-25-1878)
Bolton, Cornelius to Matilda Steel 12-28-1854
Bolton, Daniel to Elizabeth Higs 9-14-1851
Bolton, Henry to Lucy Bolton 8-9-1874 (8-20-1874)
Bolton, John to Elizabeth Branama 6-2-1872
Bolton, Louis to Sarah Wilson 3-27-1876 (3-30-1876)
Booth, C. H. to Nancy Huntsinger 10-20-1881 (10-21-1880?)
Booth, Calvin H. to Lucinda Cooper 8-21-1856
Booth, Wiley S. to Nancy Baker 7-28-1858
Boruff, Henry to Martha Jackson 10-14-1850 (10-15-1850)
Boruff, William to Caroline Curnutt 4-10-1850 (4-11-1850)
Boshears, Geo. to Roda Reynolds 2-26-1876
Boshears, Jeremiah to Elly Ann Miller 8-19-1839 (8-20-1839)
Boshears, Jeremiah to Polly Wilhoite 12-22-1871 (12-23-1871)
Boshears, Jeremiah to Sarah Malicoat 6-3-1844
Boshears, Levi to Elisabeth Keith 3-12-1865 (no return)
Boshears, Sterling to Catherine Wilson 1-6-1880 (1-7-1880)
Boshears, William to Elizabeth Adkins 3-13-1845 (3-15-1845)
Boswell, James to Cintha Honeycutt 7-3-1841 (7-7-1841)
Boulin, Berry to Vestia Brown 10-28-1847
Boulton, Hiram to Rhoda Standley 10-22-1840
Boulton, Jos. to Elizabeth Booth 7-11-1862 (7-12-1862)
Boulton, Josiah to Elizabeth Sandfill 1-22-1846
Bowers, Daniel to Keziah Hamblin 5-2-1839
Bowlin, G. W. to Elisabeth Carr 11-9-1878
Bowlin, Isaac to Eliza Young 6-23-1872
Bowlin, Isom to Mary Provence 12-15-1874
Bowlin, Samuel to Lucinda Carr 9-11-1871 (9-12-1871)
Bowlin, Samuel to M. A. McCully 2-7-1880

Bowling, Enoch to Rachal Ivey 7-31-1868 (8-20-1868)
Bowlinger, Eli to Nancy J. Canon 11-26-1880 (11-30-1880)
Bowlinger, Wm. to Polly Curnutt 4-4-1847 (no return)
Bowman, Elias to Nancey Douglass 3-5-1840
Bowman, Jas. O. to Ruminta J. Hilton 10-31-1848
Bowman, Lewis to Martha Smith 12-5-1878 (12-15-1878)
Bowman, William to Susan Perkins 10-30-1865
Bowman, Winston to Nancy Smith 2-19-1874
Bowman, Wm. to Susan McLain 5-2-1843 (no return)
Boyd, Cade to Amanda Caiin 4-6-1868 (4-17-1868)
Boyed, Charles to Eliza McNeal 9-16-1872 (10-13-1872)
Boyer, John E. to Nancey F. Stringer 12-20-1842
Braden, Cornelius to Nancy Smith 12-9-1851 (12-30-1851)
Braden, George to Ann P. Smith 11-5-1856
Braden, James B. to Martha Frances Robinson 9-27-1878 (9-29-1878)
Braden, Silas to Hannar Burriss 9-26-1874 (10-4-1874)
Braden, Warren to Emly Lay 8-8-1874 (8-13-1874)
Bradin, Warren to Emmaly Lay 8-10-1874 (8-13-1874)
Bradley, W. M. to Sophia Taylor 1-11-1880
Branham, Alexander to Louisa Sprowls 9-8-1878
Branham, Hillery F. to Susan Emaline Ayres 12-3-1865
Branham, James M. to Mary Ann Wilburn 7-18-1859
Branham, Johnathan to Elizabeth Wilson 3-28-1874 (4-5?-1874)
Branham, William R. to Nancy Row 2-22-1872
Brannum, J. C. to Elzira Byrd 9-5-1868 (9-6-1868)
Branscome, T. W. to Sarah A. Rogers 10-5-1864 (10-6-1864)
Branstler, Frederick to Melinda Wilson 3-6-1855
Brantly, A. Luther to Susan Bailey 12-16-1876 (12-17-1876)
Brantly, Benjamin to Netty Loy 1-25-1855 (no return)
Brantly, Joseph to Tinny Hill 8-10-1849 (8-16-1849)
Brantly, Thomas to Margarett Stephens 1-24-1851 (1-30-1851)
Bratcher, A. S. to Elizabeth Miller 9-4-1857 (9-17-1857)
Bratcher, Amos to Elizabeth Goin 12-24-1842 (1-1-1843)
Bratcher, Andrew to Martha J. Housley 11-7-1865 (11-9-1865)
Bratcher, B. F. to Jennie V. Robinson 2-28-1879 (3-6-1879)
Bratcher, Benj. F. to Nancy Y. Cain 2-4-1852 (2-12-1852)
Bratcher, John C. to Martha Gray 8-21-1840 (8-25-1840)
Bratcher, William to Margaret Roach 9-8-1869
Bratcher, Wm. to Rachel Patterson 9-1-1853 (no return)
Brather, Thomas to Sallie Agee 11-12-1871 (11-30-1871)
Bray, J. Van to Nancy Manhollon 12-13-1880
Bray, William P. to Selvana Bryant 1-7-1881
Briant, Paskel G. to Margaret Adkins 3-15-1838
Brides, Wm. to Lockey Hill 1-16-1851 (no return)
Bridgeman, O. P. to S. J. Owens 5-8-1853 (no return)

Bridges, Andrew to Permelia Hill 3-14-1855 (3-15-1855)
Bridges, Elijaha to Margaret Ann Miller 12-20-1872 (12-26-1872)
Bridges, Isaac to Elizabeth Miller 2-20-1874 (2-22-1874)
Bridges, R. H. to Serrepta Lawson 11-12-1845 (no return)
Bridges, William to Delila Nelson 8-3-1840 (8-4-1840)
Bridges, William to Mary A. Johnson 5-29-1872
Bridges, Wm. H. to Catharian Foust 9-22-1875 (9-24-1876)
Bridmon, S. D. to Mary A. H. Queener 12-26-1844
Briton, Archibald to Martha Woods 6-20-1841
Brock, John to Rebecca Langley 9-6-1842 (9-7-1842)
Brock, William to Sarah Newman 4-5-1845 (4-6-1845)
Brockus, Joseph P. to Mary Yount 10-31-1856
Brogan, John to Mary J. Sharp ?-25-1859
Broils, Michael to Rachael Siler 8-31-1856
Brooks, George to Barbary Abbet 4-30-1871
Brooks, George to Sarah Brathcer 1-6-1844
Brooks, John I. to Mary Hatherly 11-26-1856 (11-27-1856)
Brooks, Thomas to Elizabeth Lay 1-31-1844
Brooks, William to Mary Smith 11-18-1854 (11-19-1854)
Broughton, O. J. to Martha Cain 6-14-1840 (6-15-1840)
Brown, Benjamin H. to Harriett H. Swan 4-6-1843
Brown, David to Sarah Phillips 4-4-1850
Brown, Eli to Kitty Gross 1-27-1853
Brown, Eli to Martha Neill 2-20-1855 (no return)
Brown, F. L. to Mary Bullock 6-16-1864 (no return)
Brown, Francis M. to Nancy E. Delk 11-29-1869
Brown, G. W. to America Alder 9-6-1847 (9-12-1847)
Brown, G. W. to Catharine Heatherly 12-11-1859 (12-15-1859)
Brown, George W. to Nancy J. Dossett 4-14-1877 (4-15-1877)
Brown, George W. to Rachal A. Compton 5-30-1872 (6-3-1872)
Brown, Hamilton to Sally Phillips 8-23-1846
Brown, Harison to Lucy Stanfill 7-20-1871
Brown, Henry D. to Mary Ann Flatford 12-14-1870 (12-25-1870)
Brown, Irvin to Sarah Smith 11-15-1868
Brown, James S. to Levicy Lay 8-9-1858 (5?-20-1858)
Brown, James to Anna Cannon 1-19-1865 (1-26-1865)
Brown, John H. to Elizabeth Briton 8-10-1857
Brown, John to Mary Ann Heatherly 12-21-1868 (12-31-1868)
Brown, Joseph D. to Jane Keeny 1-15-1849 (1-28-1849)
Brown, Joseph L. S. to Mary C. Perkins 1-1-1871
Brown, Joseph to Bitha Baker 12-12-1876
Brown, Leroy to Elvina Douglass 8-22-1846 (8-23-1846)
Brown, Saml. to Celia Walker 5-16-1852 (6-3-1852)
Brown, Saml. to Elizabeth Lynch 12-3-1860 (12-6-1860)
Brown, Samuel to Mary Graves 3-1-1838 (5-29-1838)

Brown, Samuel to Mary Rogers 5-19-1871 (5-21-1871)
Brown, Taylor W. to Sarah A. Madden 1-7-1874
Brown, Thomas to Catherine Honeycut 12-10-1839
Brown, Wm. to Nancy Carroll 10-21-1846 (10-13?-1846)
Brown, Wm. to Patsy Hutson 7-14-1858 (7-15-1858)
Broyles, Aaron to Lavina Thomas 10-5-1842 (10-6-1842)
Broyles, Aaron to Marya Faulkner 3-21-1850
Broyles, Andrew F. to Sarah Douglas 9-27-1874
Broyles, Felix to Abigal Grant 5-2-1870 (5-3-1870)
Broyles, Felix to Emeline Johnson 1-22-1855 (1-25-1855)
Broyles, George to Biddy Lawson 9-14-1863
Broyles, James L. to Lydia Lovely 12-21-1878 (12-25-1878)
Broyles, James S. to Nancy Smith 3-13-1873
Broyles, John to Susannah Smith 8-29-1876
Broyles, Michael to Martha Centres 9-16-1862
Broyles, Riley to Rachael R. Morgan 10-5-1861 (10-6-1861)
Broyles, Samuel to Eliza Thomas 8-14-1851
Broyles, William Jr. to Rebecca Baird 8-19-1875
Broyles, William to Rhoda Douglass 11-10-1842
Broyls, George P. to Martha Gayler 10-7-1860
Bruce, Edly N. to Jane Orice 12-20-1860
Bruce, Heseckiah to Nancy Walden 2-23-1863 (3-5-1863)
Bruce, John to Sarah Davis 3-31-1864
Bruce, Robert to Mariah J. Bolton 5-29-1859
Bruce, William to A. E. Bridgman 3-6-1856 (no return)
Bruce, William to Cinthy Ann Mapin 6-9-1838 (6-19-1838)
Bruce, Willis to Nancy Bridgeman 12-12-1850
Brumet, L. lt to Harriet Hampton 3-11-1858 (3-12-1858)
Brummett, G. W. to Nancy Carver 12-19-1878 (12-24-1878)
Brummitt, Joseph to Cintha Stanly 10-4-1874
Brummitt, Wm. to Sarah Standler 5-5-1850
Bryant, A. J. to Susanah Lovate 11-2-1851
Bryant, Abel to Eliza Duncan 12-29-1846
Bryant, Critendon to Martha Murray 11-17-1872
Bryant, Francis F. to Malinda Skinner 3-10-1850
Bryant, George to Lydia Pennington 11-4-1838 (11-11-1838)
Bryant, Isaac to Elizabeth Hatfield 3-21-1850
Bryant, Joel to Nancy Siler 9-24-1850
Bryant, John to Caytharnie Jackson 2-29-1858 (2-24-1858)
Bryant, John to Elizabeth Los 1-11-1839
Bryant, John to Parley Hill 4-27-1850 (5-2-1850)
Bryant, Pascal to Martha Nix 3-7-1856
Bryant, R. A. to Mary McCoy 2-25-1880
Bryant, R. to K. Wilson 6-27-1878
Buck, Burton to Lavina Miller 11-20-1843 (no return)

Buckley, S. S. to Nancy Green 1-3-1844 (1-4-1844)
Buckner, Wm. to Angeline Myers 11-8-1870 (11-17-1870)
Bullock, Aaron to Nancy Mozier 3-1-1849 (no return)
Bullock, Francis to Milley Curnutt 9-12-1863 (9-13-1863)
Bullock, Wm. B. to Barbara Hatmaker 10-12-1865 (no return)
Bunch, George to Sarah Rains 10-5-1856
Bunch, Isaac to Polley McGee 11-26-1840
Bunch, James to Vilotty Hankins 12-17-1873
Bunch, John M. Ellet to Elizabeth Bolen 3-1-1873
Bunch, John V. to Sarah A. Rains 8-19-1858
Bunch, Nelson to Martha Corta 8-15-1864
Bunch, Peral to Elizabeth Lawson 9-2-1877
Bunch, Samuel to Elizabeth Mouhollon 7-6-1877
Bunch, Wm. to Elizabeth Rains 9-19-1857
Bunet, George to Marget Lawson 2-19-1880
Burge, Andrew J. to Ann J. Longman 4-19-1852
Burge, Michaele to Elizabeth Phillips 9-23-1859 (9-25-1859)
Burge, Preston to Clara Hewith 2-2-1847 (2-9-1847)
Burge, Samuel to Polly Luallen 3-18-1844 (3-21-1844)
Burnett, Richd. to Flora Wilson 11-11-1847 (no return)
Burrass, G. P. to M. A. Disney 3-1-1878 (3-3-1878)
Burrass, General P. to Betcy Hatmaker 5-18-1862 (5-25-1862)
Burrass, J. F. to S. J. Reynolds 11-23-1878 (12-29-1878)
Burrass, Jacob to Charity Riggs 11-19-1875
Burrass, John to N. J. Huckeby 9-4-1869 (9-13-1869)
Burrass, William to Sarah K. Fleming 11-10-1849
Burrass, Wm. L. to Catharine Trail 2-26-1858 (2-21?-1858)
Burress, Alfred to Elisabeth Carroll 8-9-1879 (8-10-1879)
Burris, Bluford to Frances Tally 12-7-1844 (12-8-1844)
Burris, Elijah to Polley Jarmana 10-9-1839 (10-13-1839)
Burris, Henry to Polly Gray 1-17-1843 (1-19-1843)
Burton, John to Evarilla Taylor 1-9-1869
Burton, W. A. to R. A. Stokes 12-17-1863 (no return)
Butler, Doctor C. to Sarah J. Monday 7-12-1865 (no return)
Butler, James G. to Lucinda Turner 1-4-1872 (1-6-1872)
Butler, John M. to Sarah Braden 8-17-1853 (8-18-1853)
Butler, Joseph to Mary Burk 12-27-1878
Butler, Robert to T. M. Leach 5-19-1877 (5-20-1877)
Butram, Wesly to Polly Carson 2-21-1847
Buttar, Joseph to Hulda Miller 12-22-1880 (12-23-1880)
Byrge, Davaid to Sarah Phillip 5-5-1877
Byrge, G. W. to Mary Byrge 9-27-1879 (8-28-1879)
Caddell, J. E. to M. E. McGee 10-20-1878
Caddell, P. C. to Lucinda Moses 1-18-1862
Caddell, William to Louisa Moses 1-1-1846

Cain, Ayres M. to Nancy Kincaid 5-22-1861 (6-6-1861)
Cain, Jack to Mollie Richardson 9-20-1871 (9-21-1871)
Cain, Russell M. to O. L . Dossett 9-22-1879 (9-25-1879)
Cain, William to Nancy Smith 5-29-1848 (5-3-1848)
Cain, Wm. to Julia Mosingo 9-11-1879
Caldwell, Wm. to H. M. McNew 6-29-1880 (7-1-1880)
Cammer, John to Haney Jane Wieric 12-14-1872 (12-24-1872)
Campbell, Anbel to Relda Anderson 9-29-1858
Campbell, G. W. to Elisabeth Douglass 4-9-1875
Campbell, H. C. to Hannah Piles 10-23-1867 (12-25-1867)
Campbell, Isom to Nancy E. Brooks 2-16-1865
Campbell, Jackson to Elizabeth Perkins 1-18-1844
Campbell, James D. to Catharine Petree 6-16-1852 (6-17-1852)
Campbell, James to Barbory Glenn 10-8-1840
Campbell, James to Mary D. Sprowls 6-3-1877
Campbell, Jas. D. to C. A. Nilson 9-7-1841 (no return)
Campbell, Jere to Lucinda Bronham 4-30-1855 (4-31?-1855)
Campbell, John to Fanny Rookard 12-27-1849
Campbell, John to Sarah Duncain 4-3-1845
Campbell, Jos. to Mary Douglass 11-26-1843
Campbell, Joseph to Eliza Perkins 2-12-1846
Campbell, Joseph to Stena Nelson 5-5-1840 (no return)
Campbell, Labin to Elizabeth Davis 10-8-1871
Campbell, Tom N. to Catherine Sharp 6-14-1839
Campbell, Wiet to Mary A. Chadwell 11-10-1864
Campbell, William to Sarah Graves 4-21-1842
Campbell, Wm. to Catharine Queener 8-26-1846
Campbell, Wm. to Elizabeth Russell 2-22-1854 (2-23-1854)
Canada, Martin to Rachal Word 2-9-1841 (no return)
Canaday, Solomon to Mary A. Ward 2-3-1857
Canady, Sterling to Elizabeth Ward 10-20-1860 (11-21-1860)
Canady, Wesly to Mima Pattersons 2-10-1855 (2-12-1855)
Cannen, Jackson to Elizabeth D. J. Gross 3-20-1859
Cannon, Jackson to Ageline Tillery 7-18-1839 (7-21-1839)
Cannon, James to Martha Tuder 10-8-1838
Cannon, William to Louisa Craig 8-11-1840 (no return)
Cannon, Wm. E. to Martha E. Graham 12-25-1865
Cantern, James P. to Margaret A. Masingo 11-9-1878 (11-10-1878)
Carne?, Jacob to Rachel Miller 10-16-1880
Carner, Charles R. to Syrena S. Young 10-13-1870
Carnutt, Jno. M. to Louisa Albright 12-31-1844 (no return)
Caroll, King to Louisa Arther 6-8-1876 (6-11-1876)
Caroll, Sampson to Mary Jane Ward 2-14-1876
Carpenter, Jeremiah to Martha Harpe 12-9-1866
Carpenter, John H. to Louisa Elkins 2-20-1865

Carr, Richd. to Nancy Ann Marshall 3-16-1852 (3-18-1852)
Carrell, James M. to Manervey L. Morgan 11-6-1873
Carroll, Alexander to Pattsy Emery 2-14-1845
Carroll, Asa to Elizabeth Kennedy 5-12-1880 (May 1880)
Carroll, B. to Comfort Hall 12-4-1864 (no return)
Carroll, Daniel W. to Mary A. Rollins 2-2-1873
Carroll, Harrison to Mary Amanda Rogers 12-5-1868 (12-6-1868)
Carroll, Hickman to Elizabeth McCulley 7-1-1842 (no return)
Carroll, James W. to Nancy York 7-24-1853
Carroll, Jno. to Nancy Patison 9-1-1845 (no return)
Carroll, Martin to Morning Willburn 8-24-1854
Carroll, Maticin to Biddy Holt 7-15-1864 (7-17-1864)
Carroll, Noah to Mary Miller 4-9-1880 (4-18-1880)
Carroll, Pery to E. Bullock 8-13-1877 (8-16-1877)
Carroll, Robert to Mary Suter 5-15-1853
Carroll, Samuel to Ann Pebley 3-23-1842
Carroll, Shered to Patty York 2-7-1862 (2-8-1862)
Carroll, Wm. Watson to Melvina Conner 5-12-1879 (5-14-1879)
Carroll, Wm. to Catharine York 8-6-1852 (8-8-1852)
Carson, James to F. E. Smith 12-6-1847 (no return)
Carson, John to Melvina Ford 6-1-1870 (6-2-1870)
Carter, James to Kisiah Reynolds 10-2-1851
Carter, William to Elizabeth Adkins 10-26-1841
Carver, James to Alcey Jackson 3-14-1840 (no return)
Carver, Mark to Telitha Lovely 8-2-1878 (12-26-1878)
Carver, William to Eliza Burriss 1-28-1856
Carver, William to Nancy Hatmaker 1-3-1846 (1-4-1846)
Carver?, Elijah to Eliza Steel 8-29-1842
Cary, Champ to Mima Moore 7-14-1877
Casey, L. S. to Luisa Car 3-13-1878
Casey, Leonard to Tiladay Tary 7-29-1850
Cassell, John to Martha Oaks 3-24-1855 (3-29-1855)
Cassteel, Daniel to Vicy Reeves 7-29-1879
Cates, Andrew to Nancy J. Ivey 3-3-1869 (3-6-1869)
Cates, Daniel to Elizabeth Riggs 3-19-1858 (3-20-1858)
Cates, John to Jane Dixon 9-17-1864 (no return)
Caudell, John to Emily J. Atkins 12-27-1849
Cavett, William E. to Allice Melton 12-26-1874
Caywood, Daniel to Sarah E. Rawson 4-4-1864 (4-7-1864)
Chadwell, David C. to Mary Ann Murray 5-26-1859
Chadwell, James P. to Permelia A. Bruce 3-23-1865
Chadwell, Peter to Martha Gross 12-24-1879 (12-25-1879)
Chadwell, Samuel H. to Nancy Bruce 5-24-1868
Chadwell, William to Martha Teague 10-10-1874
Chamber, Abraham to Silvaniah A. Lovet 1-19-1860

Chambers, Dan'l. to Phebe Phillips 3-5-1844 (5-14-1844)
Chambers, Obediah to Martha Bird 1-15-1881 (1-16-1881)
Chambers, Thomas to Jane Owens 9-2-1838
Champlin, Wm. A. to Charity R Hogan 9-30-1851
Chandler, J. S. to Mary J. Powers 7-17-1879
Chapman, Clem to Nancy Jane Roach 2-14-1861
Chapman, Henry to T. E. Cantrell 2-16-1878
Chapman, James A.? to Mary Jane Maupin 9-5-1870 (9-9-1870)
Chapman, James to Eliza Hale 3-6-1846 (3-8-1846)
Chapman, Jno. to Orpha Riggs 8-19-1843 (8-30-1843)
Chapman, Joel to Margarett Woods 2-8-1841 (2-9-1841)
Chapman, John to Lucinda Burrass 5-8-1856
Chapman, Robert to Polly Mallicoat 4-11-1850 (no return)
Chapman, Thomas to Milly Ann Smith 10-1-1851 (10-2-1851)
Chapman, W. H. to Elisa E. Stephens 12-10-1875 (12-12-1875)
Chapman, W. to Susan Leach 1-11-1855 (no return)
Chapman, Wm. to Catharine A. Muzingo 2-21-1851 (2-26-1851)
Chapman, Wm. to M. Wilson 8-27-1856 (8-28-1856)
Chaudoin, Francis to Elizabeth Heath 4-11-1842 (no return)
Chavis, John to Nancy Tate 8-20-1844 (no return)
Chavis, Sterlilng to M. Lumpkins 12-5-1851 (12-7-1851)
Chaviss, Peter to Amy Ivins 10-17-1857
Chesterson, Jno. L. to Martha Wilhite 4-10-1845
Childress, J. C. to Mary Jane Dossett 8-14-1878 (8-25-1878)
Childress, P. C. to Johannah Foley 9-21-1875
Childress, R. L. to Ellen Muzingo 3-19-1855 (3-22-1855)
Childress, Robert C. to Elisabeth Smith 10-12-1865 (10-13-1865)
Childress, Robert C. to Mary Lawson 3-16-1859 (no return)
Childress, William to Nancey Laugherty 1-9-1839
Childress, Wm. L. to Ann Crosswhite 6-1-1863 (no return)
Childriss, Elisha to Lucey Meaders 4-21-1842 (4-25-1842)
Childriss, Thomas to Mariah Martin 3-19-1846
Chittwood, Jonathan to Sephrony Ross 2-9-1850 (2-10-1850)
Chitwood, Andrew to Elizlabeth W. Cotten 1-5-1840
Chitwood, Julin to E#liza Province 11-27-1878
Chitwood, Pleasent to Polly Thompson 8-6-1841 (8-7-1841)
Christain, Alvis to Mary Stokes 2-26-1876 (2-27-1876)
Church, Joseph R. to Olivia Heren 8-24-1872 (8-29-1872)
Church, P. W. to Lyda Herren 3-1-1872
Claiborn, C. M. to M. Queener 9-9-1870
Claiborn, C. T. to Casandria McNew 8-30-1870 (9-8-1870)
Claiborn, O. T. to Susan Butler 11-29-1875 (11-31?-1875)
Claiborn, Otat T. to Mary Smith 12-24-1841 (12-26-1841)
Claiborne, Andrew to Elizabeth Rogers 12-26-1879 (12-28-1879)
Claiborne, J. M. to Anna J. Hall 7-23-1880 (7-29-1880)

Claiborne, James to Rachel Dunn 8-24-1879 (8-28-1879)
Claibourn, R M. to Eliz. Woodson 11-28-1854 (12-14-1854)
Claibourn, Thomas to Kitty Dunbare 7-29-1868 (8-1-1868)
Clark, John to Nancy Dossett 5-14-1862
Clark, John to Nancy Riggs 8-25-1847
Clarke, Charles to Nancy Carson 12-5-1868 (12-6-1868)
Clarke, J. S. to N. E. Evans 5-20-1854 (6-25-1854)
Clarkson, John to Polly Hutson 5-22-1854 (no return)
Clear, James to Sarah Cumins 2-26-1854
Clear, William P. to Linton Philips 7-19-1874
Clements, J. B. to Hesteran Chapman 2-20-1865
Clemins, Preston to Nancy Lynch 7-8-1859 (7-10-1859)
Clepper, Thomas to Margaret Druciller Jordan 4-11-1874 (4-11-1874)
Cliborne, Ota T. to America Monday 2-4-1845 (2-9-1845)
Clotefelter, John to B. C. Tibbs 1-4-1876 (1-6-1876)
Clotfelter, Caswell to Eliza Rains 4-23-1859 (4-24-1859)
Clotfelter, Jacob S. to Sarah Bruce 9-9-1856
Clotfelter, Sampson L. to Mary J. Hatmaker 1-31-1879 (2-2-1879)
Clous, William P. to Martha Heatherly 9-22-1848 (no return)
Coal, William H. to Sarah Harman 12-3-1870 (12-5?-1870)
Cole, John C. to Hannah Hatmaker 4-?-1875 (4-16-1875)
Cole, John H. to Mary Wright 3-18-1874 (3-19-1874)
Cole, John to Cornelia Shumake 9-12-1845 (no return)
Collins, John M. to Elizabeth Baird 5-2-1874 (5-3-1874)
Collins, Joseph to Cintha Stanfill 12-27-1870
Comer, F. M. to Elisabeth J. Philips 9-28-1864 (no return)
Comer, Levi to Jennie Hutson 3-16-1879
Condry, John H. to Carley Hill 12-6-1854 (12-7-1854)
Conner, William to Elizabeth Agee 1-28-1839 (1-29-1839)
Cook, David L. to Mary Higgs 6-20-1856 (no return)
Cook, Michael to Tabitha Goleher 5-13-1847
Cook, Robt. to Matilda Haly 10-6-1851
Cook, William to Isbald Beard 9-16-1846 (9-17-1846)
Cooper, Alflred to Mary Cooper 8-16-1865
Cooper, Alfred to Martha Richardson 12-12-1859 (12-13-1859)
Cooper, Alvlis to Polley Foster 5-6-1839
Cooper, Amons to Elisa J. Hatmaker 12-31-1880 (2-24-1881)
Cooper, Andrew to Elizabeth Moser 12-31-1880 (1-9-1881)
Cooper, C. K. to Eliza H. Dossett 10-28-1872 (11-7-1872)
Cooper, Elbert to Martha J. Reeves 4-7-1860 (5-6-1860)
Cooper, Eli to Elizabeth Cooper 10-1-1867
Cooper, Eli to Polly Gross 7-11-1846 (7-12-1846)
Cooper, Ephram to Levina J. Resterson 7-12-1839 (7-13-1839)
Cooper, Fielding L. to Mary Moser 1-13-1872 (1-14-1872)
Cooper, Fountain to Leah Harris 1-28-1850 (2-3-1850)

Cooper, George to Emily Wilson 1-25-1838
Cooper, Henry to Louisa Forester 7-14-1853
Cooper, Henry to Lyia? Neil 8-9-1855
Cooper, James to Ada Burton 6-19-1847
Cooper, James to Elisabeth Maser 4-25-1876 (4-29-1876)
Cooper, Jas. B. to Katie Dagley 9-2-1876 (9-7-1876)
Cooper, John T. to Kizzie Lovely 12-23-1876 (12-25-1876)
Cooper, Joseph N. to Mary Jane Hutson 4-8-1846 (4-9-1846)
Cooper, Joseph to Jane Reynolds 10-25-1856 (10-26-1856)
Cooper, Lindsey to Mary Gaylor 12-20-1856 (12-24-1856)
Cooper, M. to M. Hatmaker 6-13-1855
Cooper, Peter to Manda Wilson 2-20-1846
Cooper, Peter to Nelly Sharp 1-13-1869 (1-28-1869)
Cooper, Peter to Rebecca Burton 1-24-1844
Cooper, Peter to Sarah J. Jordan 1-26-1858
Cooper, Reubin to Mary Dagley 7-17-1876 (8-3-1876)
Cooper, Silvester to Martha Hatmaker 10-28-1862 (no return)
Cooper, Sylvester to Harriet M. Kirkpatrick 12-14-1853 (no return)
Cooper, Thomas to Martha Thomas 12-23-1874 (12-26-1874)
Cooper, Thomas to Polley Conker 3-18-1854 (3-19-1854)
Cooper, Thos. C. to Rebecca Wilson 3-24-1879
Cooper, William to Jennettie Welch 8-4-1875 (8-5-1875)
Cooper, Wm. P. to Sally Hutson 6-12-1851 (6-19-1851)
Copeland, A. C. to Mary A. Stokes 12-6-1853 (12-7-1853)
Copeland, J. S. to Julia Ann Hubbard 12-17-1880
Cordie, James to Rachel Broyles 2-7-1879
Cornelius, W. E. to Susanah Broyles 2-5-1876 (2-6-1876)
Cotten, Isaac W. to Christina Jeffers 2-8-1840 (2-9-1840)
Couch, Samuel to Orlena Bird 1-10-1865
Counab?, John to Mahala Sharp 11-19-1855 (11-20-1855)
Cox, Daniel Z. to Mary Ann Zackary 5-17-1838
Cox, Elijah to Rebecca E. Jones 10-10-1870
Cox, George to Martha Wilson 12-18-1872 (12-20-1872)
Cox, Henry to Louisa Branum 11-8-1854 (11-16-1854)
Cox, Henry to Nancy C. Sharp 10-15-1868
Cox, Hiram to C. C. Wilson 4-17-1853 (no return)
Cox, James to Mary Wilson 9-5-1843 (9-10-1843)
Cox, Jas. to Nancey Baker 9-16-1877
Cox, Jesse to Martha McDy 4-12-1838
Cox, Jno. to Elizabeth Branham 6-10-1843 (6-11-1843)
Cox, Jonathan to Sarah Sutton 3-15-1878 (3-16-1878)
Cox, Joseph S. to Mary E. Witt 12-21-1857 (12-29-1857)
Cox, Maynard to Elizabeth Weaver 2-1-1878 (2-2-1878)
Cox, Nathan to Susan Hicks 3-23-1879
Cox, Richard to Catharine Bane 9-5-1848

Cox, William to Hannah Gray 8-3-1851 (8-4-1851)
Cox, Wm. to Cintha Archer 12-25-1869
Crabtree, Absalom to Jane Cooper 11-1-1845
Crabtree, Isaac to Sally Crabtree 2-12-1848
Crabtree, James to Bethena Claxton 5-3-1865 (6-1-1865)
Crabtree, James to Elizabeth Smith 4-25-1850 (4-26-1850)
Craig, Elisha to Sarah Maize 12-6-1878
Craig, John to C. E. Hatmaker 10-31-1877 (11-1-1877)
Craig, Reuben to Polley Cannon 3-4-1839
Craven, John to Sarah Smith 3-18-1858
Cravens, Francis to Avvey Sharp 10-29-1855 (no return)
Crawford, Benson to Locke Hope 1-3-1865
Crawford, George W. to Margaret L. Jordan 4-6-1861
Crawford, Wm. to Emly Chatman 12-31-1864 (1-3-1865)
Creekmore, Adison to Selvina Coldwell 10-30-1876
Creekmore, David H. to Elizabeth Meadors 8-13-1843
Creekmore, H. M. to M. A. Davis 7-1-1880
Creekmore, Rewcanvy? to Mary Lay 12-28-1865
Crickmore, Thomas to Mary Trammell 3-10-1850
Croley, J. J. to Thorse Ella Tye 1-29-1879
Croley, Richard C. to Nancy Hamlin 12-7-1862
Croley, Sampson to Sabry Standle 4-13-1852 (4-15-1852)
Croley, W. R. to Elizabeth Lay 3-28-1856 (3-29-1856)
Croley, Wimer to J. M. Davis 3-20-1880
Croley, Wimer to Mary Rose 9-8-1880 (no return)
Croly, Granberry to Manerva Lay 12-29-1878 (12-29-1879?)
Cross, Absalon to Sarah Massingala 12-3-1878 (12-5-1878)
Cross, Caswell to Kisiah Baker 12-16-1848 (12-21-1848)
Cross, Claiborne to Conney Barron 4-9-1880 (4-15-1880)
Cross, Georg to Angeline Huckaby 8-16-1880 (8-15?-1880)
Cross, Jacob to Cinthe M. Rutherford 8-19-1858
Cross, Jno. to Lucinda Acres 8-12-1845 (8-17-1845)
Cross, Larkin W. to Henrietta Duncan 3-22-1846 (4-2-1846)
Cross, Micager to Flemon Barron 2-17-1880 (2-19-1880)
Cross, Thomas to Catharine Adkins 12-7-1855
Crosswhite, C. L. to Elizabeteh Dabny 12-19-1853 (12-22-1853)
Crouch, Josiah to Luiza Branam 3-17-1846
Crowly, L. B. to Winney Lay 3-22-1844 (3-31-1844)
Cruchfield, H. to Rachael Collins 7-2-1860 (7-6-1860)
Crutch, Samuel to Nancy Sweat 10-30-1875
Crutchfield, H. A. to Dosia Christian 3-9-1876
Crutchfield, J. F. to Mary Ann Lawson 7-31-1871 (8-2-1871)
Crutchfield, Preston to Mary Hammon 5-23-1873
Cubirth, James to Thursy Ann McKeehan 11-26-1843
Culbirth, Joseph to Nancy Beams 12-22-1843

Curnutt, James H. to Elisabeth Lay 7-7-1862
Curnutt, Preston to Elizabeth Ann Cambell 10-15-1838 (no return)
Dabney, Cornelius to Sarah Dagley 9-9-1840
Dabney, David to Nancy Keeny 9-25-1860
Dabney, G. W. to Sarah E. Cannon 10-24-1864
Dabney, James to Melinda Reeves 10-19-1842 (10-23-1842)
Dagley, James to Joannah Roaoch 3-21-1842 (no return)
Dagley, John to Cynthia Grant 4-24-1849 (no return)
Dagley, Moses to Nancy J. Curnutt 2-16-1848 (2-2-1848)
Dagley, William to Amanda Dagly 8-26-1841
Dagly, D. to E. Parker 2-10-1855 (2-12-1855)
Dagly, James to Jane Acres 6-20-1849
Dallas, Bradford B. to Lizzie Scruggs 10-24-1880
Daniel, Peter to Lucinda Lovett 5-13-1840 (5-19-1840)
Daniels, Isaac to Mary E. Morgan 9-7-1870 (9-8-1870)
Daugherty, Moses to Nancy Phillip 3-5-1869 (1?-9-1869)
Daugherty, Paul to Angline Wilson 5-5-1877
David, John to Emily Cross 3-2-1857
David, Reubin to Anna Eliza Smiddy 3-30-1871
David, Wiley to Louisa Sparks 3-20-1880
Davis, Aaron to Elizabeth Wilhite 6?-29-1854 (ret. blank)
Davis, Aaron to Juli Ann Perkins 2-15-1879
Davis, Caswell to Faitha Devemgill 10-6-1871 (10-7-1871)
Davis, Elias to Margaret Perkins 1-21-1858
Davis, George to Martha Ross 9-7-1846
Davis, Harrison to Virginia C. Gwinn 11-16-1853
Davis, Hugh to Dorcas Trammell 9-2-1849
Davis, James 1-l. to Cynthia Stant11 4-17-1851
Davis, James to Mary Suter 9-13-1873
Davis, John to Frances Hatfield 1-29-1853
Davis, John to Pheba Ann Morgan 7-26-1873
Davis, Joseph to Elender McCidy 7-6-1843
Davis, Leroy to Malinda Hix 5-31-1855
Davis, S. B. to N. G. Lawson 2-16-1879
Davis, Thomas B. to Rosannah Hackler 12-8-1853
Davis, Wm. B. to Oliv P. Alison 4-9-1843
Davis, Wm. M. to Rachel Sentres 4-6-1865
Davis, Zachariah to Nancy McDonold 3-3-1838
Day, Jas. M. to Elizabeth Bolton 11-20-1870
Day, Joseph to Rhoda Wilson 11-28-1877 (no return)
Day, Reuben to Susan Seals 7-13-1842 (no return)
Day, William to Sarah Jackson 3-4-1871 (3-5-1871)
De Tavinier, Fredrick A. A. to Sue E. (Miss) Carey 12-5-1865
Dean, Thomas to Martha Evans 9-6-1845 (no return)
Dearee, John to Nancy Barbey 3-16-1870

Deas, Ivin to Lydia Meaders 7-4-1846
Deavenport, Ezra to Elizabeth Sego 6-27-1844
Dees, Sandford to Elisabeth Kelsoe 12-6-1864
Dekens, J. F. to Mary Ann Raines 3-25-1872
Delap, D. S. to Izabella Keeney 11-9-1870 (11-20-1870)
Delk, Allen to Elizabeth Cissle 12-6-1877
Delk, William to Permeta Lewalen 3-29-1873
Dexter, Frankling to Martha Cooper 4-18-1864
Dial, William K. to Cela Ann Roush 3-11-1874
Dickerson, Jno. to Jane Allen 3-23-1878
Dickison, George to Arminta Malone 12-13-1876 (12-14-1876)
Dickson, Hiram R. to Nancy Ann Smith 6-10-1849
Dickson, Wm. J. to Elizabeth Sharp 2-7-1856
Diew, A. J. to M. L. Bowling 10-1-1863
Diew, David to Nancy Harmon 6-7-1863 (8-8-1863)
Diew, David to Versula Harmon 5-9-1859 (1859)
Dike, Henre to Martha Pebley 2-1-1858 (12-30-1858)
Dilk, Gilbert to Prudy Fox 7-5-1848 (7-6-1848)
Dimond, Robert to Sophia Parter 12-1-1868
Disray, Wm. to Sarah Gaylor 1-29-1878 (2-1-1878)
Dixon, James to Cathrine Miller 9-17-1864 (no return)
Dixon, Nathan to Olley Quener 7-12-1879
Dorhergty, Daniel to Susan Marlow 10-11-1855 (10-14-1855)
Dossett, A. J. to Martha Ann Wiloughby 6-26-1873 (6-27-1873)
Dossett, Alfred to Ann Elliott 1-25-1838 (2-1-1838)
Dossett, Alfred to Martha J. Smith 6-30-1868 (7-2-1868)
Dossett, Alfred to Nancy Hatherly 10-2-1859
Dossett, Andrew to Issa Cain 3-11-1840 (3-15-1840)
Dossett, Daniel M. to Lucia Robins 12-22-1880 (12-23-1880)
Dossett, Edmond to Kitty Brown 9-26-1880
Dossett, Franklin to Eliza Butler 11-26-1879 (11-27-1879)
Dossett, Henderson to Lucy Hope 3-20-1855 (8-8-1855)
Dossett, John to Elizabeth McNew 1-6-1852 (1-11-1852)
Dossett, Robert to Elizabeth Wilson 9-20-1839 (9-22-1839)
Dossett, Robert to Manerva Cain 10-20-1842 (no return)
Dossett, Robert to Sarah Ann Walker 11-2-1853 (8-8-1855,sic)
Dossett, Thomas to M. B. Smith 12-14-1879 12-18-1879)
Dossett, Wm. to Eliza Hope 2-9-1843 (2-16-1843)
Dossitt, Robert to Mary Smith 10-5-1850 (10-6-1850)
Dougherty, Bird to Precy Marlow 12-23-1857 (12-24-1857)
Dougherty, Jeremiah to Ozeda Canadya 9-7-1878
Dougherty, Reubin to Elisabeth Patterson 9-1-1879
Dougherty, William to Catherine? Stout 4-12-1840
Douglas, Andrew to Elizabeth Baird 12-23-1876
Douglas, D. C. to Nancy Smith 3-7-1880

Douglas, Elias to Elisabeth Taylor 1-17-1878
Douglas, G. W. to Lucinda J. Lawson 12-7-1879
Douglas, George M. to Emly Smith 2-17-1870
Douglas, Jackson to Elizabeth Smith 10-15-1874
Douglas, Silas to Lucy Miller 8-26-1876
Douglas, T..E. to M. E. Allen 3-4-1877
Douglas, Thos. Y. to M. E. Allen 3-4-1877
Douglas, William B. to Caney Baird 6-9-1872
Douglas, William to Esther Davis 8-9-1880
Douglass, Aaron to Nancy J. Creekmore 12-30-1875
Douglass, George M. to Nancy Lay 2-7-1850
Douglass, George to Lucretia Wilhite 3-24-1853
Douglass, Jesse C. to Susan Sawyers 3-13-1853
Douglass, John B. to Catharine Meador 2-15-1858 (2-18-1858)
Douglass, John to Leah Oaks 1-29-1857
Douglass, John to Lucinda Ball 12-27-1838
Douglass, Kerby K. to Sarah Sharp 4-11-1841 (4-13-1841)
Douglass, King to Polly A. Perins 10-14-1858
Douglass, Mathew to Nancy Lay 4-16-1868
Douglass, Matthew to Hannah Baird 3-6-1851
Douglass, Saml. J. to Leah Campbell 3-25-1839
Douglass, Samuel to Eliza Carter 6-14-1840
Douglass, Samuel to Thursey Brockus 10-27-1841 (10-31-1841) [*]
Douglass, Spencer to Helon Smith 8-13-1875
Douglass, Sterlin C. to Minerva Snyder 8-11-1853
Douglass, Thomas M. to Nancy Archer 1-4-1849
Douglass, Thomas Y. to Rachel Pawley 9-9-1847
Douglass, William to Catherine Lay 7-10-1842
Douglass, William to Elizabeth Broyles 3-26-1846
Douglass, Wm. P.? to Susan Cornelius 3-19-1861 (3-28-1861)
Dowel, George to Eliza Dobson 2-19-1861
Dowel, George to Loucitty Lovet 4-25-1857 (4-26-1857)
Dowel, Henderson to Hester Lovet 1-19-1861 (1-20-1861)
Dowell, Francis to Polly Thompson 2-11-1871 (2-12-1871)
Dowell, Milton P. to Ollie Reynolds 11-5-1874
Drake, Tilmond to Nancy Roe 7-27-1846
Duckworth, Robt. to Alcy Heatherley 3-15-1864 (3-16-1864)
Duff, Wm. to Leah Murray 1-25-1844 (1-26-1844)
Duke, William to Linsey Sharp 1-4-1843 (1-8-1843)
Dula, Thomas to Elizabeth Brooks 6-13-1850
Duncain, Henry to Catharine Thompson 2-14-1845 (2-20-1845)
Duncam, John to Metilda Loyd d9-88-1841 (9-12-1841)
Duncan, Joshua to Lucey Chambers 12-13-1840 (1-2-1841?)
Duncan, Zachariah T. to Mary E. Gaylor 4-25-1879 (4-27-1879)
Duneway, John T. to Elisabeth Cathrine Thomas 6-18-1865

(6-19-1865)
Dunken, John to E. J. Wilson 8-14-1859 (8-16-1859)
Dunken, R. M. to Mary S. Thompson 12-23-1864 (sol.,no date)
Dunkin, Chesly to Martha J. Faulkner 5-19-1853
Dunkin, James to Matilda Row 6-23-1850
Dunkin, Thomas to Bethina Lumpkin 9-26-1845 (no return)
Dunn, John to Catharine Braden 11-22-1852 (11-30-1852)
Durham, Joseph to M. R. Grant 3-25-1878 (3-28-1878)
Durham, W. P. to Mary Little 11-4-1840 (no return)
Dyer, Isaac C. to Louisa Sharp 3-24-1849 (no return)
Dyer, John M. to Polly Sharp 2-26-1849 (no return)
Dyke, Wm. to Judy Ann Smiht 11-9-1851
Dyre, William to Elisabeth Carroll 2-3-1865 (2-6-1865)
Eads, Asa to Sarah Adkins 3-4-1841 (3-12-1841)
Eads, Nelson to Didama Delk 1-28-1841
Easly, John Q. A. to Elizabeth Jones 4-4-1853
East, Charles to Sarah Ford 8-16-1875 (8-17-1875)
East, J. R. to Sallee Petree 7-25-1872
East, James to Sarah Woodson 7-30-1872 (7-31-1872)
Edmonson, John B. C. to Elizabeth Owens 12-18-1865 (no return)
Elder, Moses to Charity Riggs 8-13-1856
Elison, Asa M. to Timanda J. Vannoy 10-19-1846
Elison, Jno. to Elizabeth Runnels 3-8-1844
Elison, Wm. to Elizabeth Carrot 10-27-1858 (10-28-1858)
Elkins, Alfred to Emeline M. Reeves 2-5-1856 (no return)
Elkins, David to M. J. Newport 2-19-1879 (2-23-1879)
Elkins, James to Hannah Dabney 7-5-1860 (7-6-1860)
Elkins, Jos. W. to Mary A. Riggs 2-2-1876 (2-3-1876)
Elkins, Joseph to Polly Hart 1-5-1852 (12-15-1851?)
Elkins, Myratt to Mary Dean 4-11-1876
Elkins, William B. to Luiza A. Reeves 12-5-1870 (12-6-1870)
Ellington, David to Rebecca Martin 2-27-1838 (no return)
Elliott, Frank to Lucy Sweat 12-24-1878 (12-26-1878)
Elliott, John to Eliza Jane Baily 1-19-1838
Ellis, Zachariah to Elizabeth Myers 10-5-1875
Ellison, Asa M. to Sarah Reynolds 10-26-1858
Ellison, Berry to Titha Boriff 2-16-1855 (no return)
Ellison, Gilbert to Charlotte Reynolds 5-6-1854
Ellison, John to Julian Boyers 6-7-1840
Elmore, John to Harriot J. Scott 9-15-1857
Embry, Benjamin to Sarah Evans 10-9-1875 (10-10-1875)
Engle, Elex to Margret Hembre 11-30-1876
Engle, Shanklin to Matilda J. Eliott 9-30-1844
Fipps, John to Elisabeth Kneedum 1-19-1865
Flatford, David to Martha Henderson 3-27-1853 (3-28-1853)

Flatford, John to Lucinda Craig 111-1848 (11-2-1848)
Flatford, Levan to Elizabeth Lay 11-11-1847 (no return)
Fleming, George to M. J. Queener 1-27-1855
Fleming, S. C. to M. A. Stokes 8-27-1853 (8-28-1853)
Fletcher, George to Nancy Malone 1-2-1869
Floyed, Soloman to Oly Blankenship 5-17-1868
Foister, Daniel to Elizabeth Mazingoe 11-13-1857 (11-15-1857)
Foley, Even to Malinda Snider 8-19-1865 (8-24-1865)
Foley, Greenbury to Ann Ingle 10-7-1838
Foley, Hugh to Nancy Duncan 5-18-1854
Foly, Green to Rachael Jones 12-4-1851 (11?-4-1851)
Foly, Green to Rachael Jones 1851 (no return)
Forbes, D. J. to Martha A. Leach 3-27-1865 (4-24-1865)
Ford, Aaron to Nancy McKeehan 7-12-1855 (no return)
Ford, Archable to Francis Prater 4-5-1881 (4-7-1881)
Ford, Boon to S. J. Stokes 1-8-1878 (1-10-1878)
Ford, Cravans to Eliza Jane Burris 2-5-1874
Ford, D. to Clary Housley 4-24-1868 (4-30-1868)
Ford, Daniel M. to Levina Parker 7-20-1868 (9-24-1868)
Ford, Isaac N. to M. T. Hampton 1-7-1854 (no return)
Ford, Isaac to Harriet Griffin 8-3-1847
Ford, Isaac to Margeret Ivy 3-12-1878
Ford, James to Ann Ford 11-3-1840 (11-8-1840)
Ford, James to Elizabeth Tuttle 4-28-1865 (no return)
Ford, James to Jane Robins 10-1-1880
Ford, John C. to Ann Petree 6-20-1844 (June 1844)
Ford, John to Nancy Henson 3-23-1871
Ford, Randolph to Barbara Calahan 12-3-1878 (12-4-1878)
Ford, Wilson to Lucinda Douglas 11-4-1871 (11-5-1871)
Forgeson, Peter H. to Cordelia Prichard 2-11-1873
Forister, James to Alseye Miller 10-7-1878
Foster, Maraul to Rhoda Caslin 11-27-1840
Foust, Christopher to Susan Nelson 12-21-1840 (no return)
Foust, Daniel to Esther Strader 2-27-1840 (3-5-1840)
Foust, Danil to A. Malaly 4-12-1878 (4-13-1878)
Foust, John L. to Nancy Brooks 2-6-1875
Fox, Franklin to Rosanah Brown 1-25-1857
Fox, Joseph to Hannah Beams 1-18-1846
Fox, William to Milly Slatton 12-30-1852
Frank, Sweat to Mary Williamson 12-25-1856
Franklin, Gray to Mary Clepper 1-12-1877 (1-14-1877)
Frederick, John to Feroby Woods 11-30-1859
Fredrick, John to Eliza E. Ellison 6-26-1864
Freeman, C. M. to Mary Herron 12-9-1869 (12-12-1869)
Freeman, H. L. to Mahala Brookes 8-24-1840 (8-30-1840)

Freeman, James to Elizabeth Mazingo 7-28-1871 (7-30-1871)
Fuller, Fielding to Elizabeth Bryant 5-18-1875
Fulps, Alex. to Nancy Kirk 5-26-1855 (5-27-1855)
Gad, John S. to Mary Abner 2-5-1851
Gailer, Thomas to Nancy Gibson 3-16-1850 (3-17-1850)
Gailer, Thomas to Susannah Harmon 8-30-1849
Gailor, Aaron to Delila Baird 1-12-1854
Gailor, Powell to Anna Landrum 6-12-1868 (6-20-1868)
Galer, Aaron to Easter Hicks 5-16-1869
Gallihor, Joseph to Feby Ingland 12-4-1864 (no return)
Gardener, James H. to Surelda Bennett Elkins 9-5-1872
Garner, Pleasant H. to Mary Jane Lindsay 2-5-1881 (2-6-1881)
Gatliff, J. W. to E. D. Goodin 1-27-1853
Gatliff, Milton to Sarilda Cummins 7-22-1842
Gatliff, Moses to Elizabeth Stanfill 10-4-1842
Gatliff, Samuel to Frances Tye 8-30-1877
Gayler, Aron to Susan Malindy Jordan 8-28-1873
Gayler, John L. to Rachel Perkins 8-17-1873
Gayler, Wm. to Sarah Dabney 9-15-1860 (9-16-1860)
Gaylor, Aaron to Sarah E. Smith 2-6-1876
Gaylor, Christopher to Martha Waldene 2-9-1851
Gaylor, Jesse to Policy Harmon 11-30-1871 (11?-1-1871)
Gaylor, Joseph to Biddy Hatfield 10-10-1876 (10-11-1876)
Gaylor, Paul to Mary Gearman 3-4-1878
Gaylor, Reuben to Martha Gaylor 6-29-1854
Gaylor, Thos. to Sarah J. Slover 10-12-1876
Gaylor, W. R. to Martha Burrass 2-4-1874 (2-5-1874)
Gaylor, Wm. R. to Martha Burrass 2-4-1874
Gentry, Adison to Rebecca Rice 1-6-1845 (1-12-1845)
Gibbert, Lewis to Elizabeth McCulley 10-6-1858 (10-7-1858)
Gibbs, Robert to Nancy J. Wilson 10-2-1879
Gibson, Cade to Creesy Evans 9-12-1874
Gibson, F. M. to Mary Broyles 3-13-1865 (no return)
Gibson, Georg to Sarah Hix 9-24-1860
Gibson, George to Nancy Campbell 12-23-1853
Gibson, Henry to Amanda Landon 4-19-1870
Gibson, Henry to Cynthia Broyles 12-11-1854
Gibson, J. C. to Rebecca Lay 7-7-1876
Gibson, James T. to Amah C. Pogue 7-12-1870
Gibson, James to Catharine Douglass 4-4-1855
Gibson, Prior to Charlotta Archer 1-14-1858
Gibson, Stephen to Elizabeth Smith 4-9-1843
Gibson, Zackry to Emeline Lawson 12-9-1872
Gilbert, Haywood to Nancey Clark 9-15-1840
Ginings, Thos. to M. E. Ball 6-8-1878

Givier?, Benjamin to Jane Wilson 1-19-1841 (no return)
Glenn, Madison to Lyda Harnass 9-9-1870 (9-11-1870)
Glenn, Matison to Elizabeth Miller 5-17-1840 (5-18-1840)
Glenn, Wm. to Sarah Ivey 7-8-1880 (7-10-1880)
Goad, John to Lucretia Phillips 9-11-1838
Godsey, Sam to Liddy Miller 3-4-18876 (3-5-1876)
Goin, Alvis to Caroline Miller 9-24-1873 (9-28-1873)
Goin, Isham to Minerva Ann Soaps 8-1-1851 (8-10-1851)
Goin, Milton to Pheba Smith 5-30-1857 (5-31-1857)
Goin, Preston to D. A. King 33-10-1841 (no return)
Goin, Win. to Catharine Carroll 3-3-1845 (no return)
Goins, Alvis to Manda Kimerin 12-12-1878 (12-15-1878)
Goins, Benjamin Franklin to Sarah Smith 8-4-1871 (8-6-1871)
Goins, Granvill to Lucy McGlothlin 9-25-18875 (10-4-1875)
Goins, Isham to E. Low 8-31-1864 (no return)
Goins, Isham to Malvina large 8-31-1864 (9-1-1864)
Goins, John to Mary A. Ashworth 6-29-1872 (6-30-1872)
Goins, Marshall to Martha Dossett 4-17-1876 (4-20-1876)
Goins, Thos. to Elizabeth Smith 1-1-1880
Goins, Wiatt to Pheobea Goins 8-29-1868
Goodman, Albert A. to Mary J. Lovitt 3-24-1880 (3-25-1880)
Goodman, Jesse to Ceily Candy 10-9-1856 (exec.,no date)
Goodman, Robert to Martha J. Richardson 10-9-1876
Gossadge, Joel to Mahala Plaster 9-9-1845 (9-13-1845)
Gragory, Green to Catharine McKehan 2-22-1871
Graham, G. W. to Elisabeth Powel 4-11-1865 (12-3-1865)
Graham, Homer to Lidda Cravens 10-3-1865
Graham, Horace to Margaret Neal 4-6-1879 (4-3?-1879)
Graham, John to Mary E. Hope 11-3-1870
Graham, Lucius P. to Elisabeth Owens 12-2-1865
Graham, Willie to Clarissa Montgomer 7-27-1842 (8-21-1842)
Grant, Harvey to Helen Lay 8-23-1850 (8-29-1850)
Grant, Henry to Rebecca Johnson 5-23-1863 (5-10-1863)
Grant, J. C. to N. C. Haggard 12-19-1876 (12-21-1876)
Grant, James H. Jr. to Lucy A. Standley 114-1865 (11-22-1865)
Grant, James H. to Catharine Corner 4-2-1855 (no return)
Grant, John P. to Sarah Jones 5-2-2872
Grant, Rufus to Lucy Parker 3-26-1845 (no return)
Grant, William to M. E. Ridener 10-17-1880
Gray, Edmon to Elizabeth Richardson 10-8-1859 (10-9-1859)
Gray, Edmond to Polly Wilson 11-13-1841 (11-14-1841)
Gray, James to Elizabeth Loy 8-8-1851 (no return)
Gray, James to Mary Tally 10-17-1844 (10-23-1844)
Gray, Jasper to Helon Harris 1-13-1859
Gray, Joseph to Nancy Farmer 11-11-1841 (11-14-1841)

Gray, Joseph to Rebecca Sweaton 8-17-1865
Gray, Robert to Francis Mallicoat 9-6-1839 (no return)
Gray, Thomas W. to Hannah H. Gross 12-7-1850 (12-15-1850)
Gray, Thos. B. to Sarah Vinsant 10-28-1878 (10-24?-1878)
Grayham, Jasper to Katy Perkins 9-29-1875
Grayham, John B. to Mary J. Wilson 7-30-1860
Green, John B. to Nancy Lavzee 12-13-1859
Green, John F. to Sarah Carroll 11-12-1858
Green, R. F. to E. J. Wallace 8-26-1857
Green, R. F. to Mary J. Adkins 5-15-1868 (4?-16-1868)
Green, Richard to Mary Jane Hutson 7-16-1845 (no return)
Green, Robert to Elisabeth Ford 5-17-1879 (5-18-1879)
Green, Wm. to Emlie Thompson 11-11-1876 (11-12-1876)
Green, Wm. to M. C. Longmire 11-10-1860 (11-15-1860)
Green, Wm. to Mary Jane Wilson 3-31-1871 (4-2-1871)
Greenlee, Joseph R. to Pheobe Casadad 6-21-1872 (6-22-1872)
Greenway, John to Mary A. Brown 8-1-1864 (8-15-1864)
Greer, Henry H. to Margaret Stanfill 6-10-1868
Greer, John T. to E. J. Brown 10-22-1853 (no return)
Gregory, Green to Mary Evans 11-18-1868
Griffeth, William A. to Nancy Jane Whitecotten 4-29-18872 (5-1-1872)
Griffries, Wm. to Melitha Miller 4-22-1850 (no return)
Griffy, Martin to Elizabeth Richardson 12-23-1848 (12-24-1848)
Griffy, Thomas to Nancy Wilson 7-18-1844
Grimes, Henry H. to Polly Flemeing 2-19-1844
Grimes, John to Nancy Y. Kincaid 6-4-1843
Gross, Abraham to Delana Webb 6-17-1865 (6-18-1865)
Gross, Amon to A. M. J. Bowlen 1-2-1858 (1-3-1858)
Gross, Amon to Elisabeth Cooper 10-3-1864 (no return)
Gross, Andrew to Mary E. Lindsay 1-23-1869 (1-24-1869)
Gross, Edmund A. to Angletta Dabney 7-9-1849 (8-4-1849)
Gross, G. W. to Louesa A. Bowling 7-20-1859 (8-24-1859)
Gross, Isaac A. to Julia C. Thomas 8-8-1857
Gross, J. T. to M. D. Smitih 4-10-1875 (4-11-1875)
Gross, Jacob W. to Jane Thomas 9-4-1852 (9-5-1852)
Gross, John to Sarah Maddin 10-14-1853 (11-15-1853)
Groves, Pleasant to Sally Hously 12-22-1849 (12-23-1849)
Guinn, Joseph B. to Emlie S. Skeins 10-11-1871
Gwin, Wm. to Elizabeth Malicote 9-9-1861 (9-11-1861)
Hackler, G. W. to Sarah Matailda Perkins 12-17-1865
Hackler, Jesse to Sarah Potter 11-26-1837
Hackler, John L. to Rachal Foby 8-23-1869
Hackler, Mathew to Sarah E. Richmond 8-26-1860
Hackler, Saml. to Martha J. Wells 1-15-1857
Hackles, Brackles to Mary Ann Booth 7-1-1852

Haggard, Warren to Lucinda Curnutt 1-5-1855 (1-16-1855)
Hale, George to Alcey Weaver 3-29-1853 (3-31-1853)
Hale, J. E. to Talitha J. Nix 8-3-1879
Hale, Jackson to Serrelda Jones 10-19-1864 (no return)
Hale, Jas. to Lucretia Dial 10-7-1876 (10-8-1876)
Hale, Kellis J. to Patsy Harris 7-16-1851 (7-17-1851)
Hale, Wm. to Margaret Hawkins 3-14-1879 (3-16-1879)
Flail, Ambrous to Barsheby Saterfield 1-26-1874 (1-27-1874)
Hall, James T. to Susan Sawyers 8-1-1874
Hall, John G. to Margaret Smith 11-27-1852 (12-2-1852)
Hall, Pulasky to Cyntha E Ridenour 9-22-1848 (no return)
Hallen, Abraham to Sarah Ann Powers 4-21-1859 (4-27-1859)
Halt, Daniel W. to Elizabeth Losson 10-16-1856
Hamblin, George W. to Martha Marlow 3-16-1873
Hamblin, George to Rebecca Smith 12-2-1852
Hamblin, J. B. to Sarah Bennett 12-27-1877
Hamblin, John to Sousan F. Sears 7-8-1879
Hamby, A. E. to Jamatte Rose 11-1880
Hamby, Abram E. to Elizabeth Chittwood 3-24-1849 (3-31-1849)
Hamby, Isaac M. to Saphrona Baird 2-13-1876
Hamby, Ivory F. to Sarah Bedkin 9-11-1842
Hamelton, Marcus to Sarah Bayless 4-12-1868 (4-13-1868)
Hamlin, George to Sarah Bryant 8-8-1875
Hamlin, Terel to Elizabeth Croly 4-15-1858
Hammons, John W. to Mary J. Murray 5-15-1879 (5-18-1879)
Hampton, Joel A. to Nancy Benit 3-21-1847 (no return)
Hampton, Reuben to Cyntha Reeves 6-1-1842 (6-2-1842)
Hancock, James to Sarah Stout 12-1848 (no return)
Hancock, William to Mary Heatherly 1-22-1842 (1-23-1842)
Hand, G. R. to Sousan R. Kelso 2-7-1865 (2-11-1865)
Hand, Geo. R. to Susan R. Keso 2-7-1865 (2-11-1865)
Harind, John T. to Melinda Sharp 1-1-1855 (1-11-1855)
Harless, John to Pothe Lynch 2-1-1880
Harless, Wm. to Elizabeth Wilson 1-6-18587 (1-11-1857)
Harmen, Samuel to Siotha? Lovet 1-1-1859 (1-2-1859)
Harmon, Aaron to Rachel Moseer 4-3-1845 (no return)
Harmon, Emanuel to Arminta E. Sharp 12-17-1877 (12-18-1877)
Harmon, H. C. to Mary E. Vittoe 10-27-1864 (no return)
Harmon, Hiram to Rebecca Roach 12-2-1853 (12-4-1853)
Harmon, Jacob to Susan Miller 7-12-1851 (7-13-1851)
Harmon, John M. to N. A. Andrews 9-24-1879 (9-26-1879)
Harmon, John to Elizlabeth Parker 12-9-1879 (12-24-1879)
Harmon, Michael to Nancy Masingal 3-15-1880 (3-19-1880)
Harmon, Saml. to Rebecca Jount 2-2-1861 (2-3-1861)
Harness, David to Elizabeth Hewitt 1-2-1840

Harness, James to Eliza Burriss 9-21-1839 (9-22-1839)
Harness, John to Jane Smither 6-25-1840
Harness, Samuel to Mary Hewett 1-14-1841
Harness, Thomas to Elizabeth Robins 12-21-1846 (12-27-1846)
Harp, James M. to L A. Richardson 6-8-1880
Harp, Joshua to Almeda More 5-21-1853
Harp, Wm. to Dolly Heslope 1-7-1861
Harrell, William to Susan Bullock 8-28-1853
Harrill, G. M. to Mattie L. McNew 12-2-1878 (12-4-1878)
Harris, John to Elmira C. Tibbs 1-19-1875 (1-21-1875)
Harris, John to Lucy Hide 2-8-1875
Harrison, Richard to Sarah Myers 10-22-1873 (10-23-1873)
Harrison, William to Mary Chatman 3-1-1865
Hart, Daniel to Nancy Bruce 12-19-1846
Hart, George to Nancy J. McKinis? 1-2-1852
Hart, John W. to Sarah A. Richardson 3-22-1854 (3-23-1854)
Hart, Thomas to Martha J. Carey 11-2-1852 (11-4-1852)
Hart, Wm. C. to Martha J. Hauskins 2-8-1850
Haskins, Samuel to Eliza Huckaby 11-25-1870 (11-26-1870)
Hatfield, Alexander to Nancy Allen 11-13-1873
Hatfield, Andrew to Polly Hatfield 5-31-1847
Hatfield, Avon to Elizabeth Sharp 2-20-1872 (2-27-1872)
Hatfield, Birl to Courtney Lavitt 12-1-1880
Hatfield, Calvin to Candia Bryant 4-29-1845
Hatfield, Calvin to Mainda Baird 4-21-1876 (4-23-1876)
Hatfield, Davis to Elizabeth Walden 10-4-1838
Hatfield, George to E. Mereda (Meridith) 12-16-1879 (12-18-1879)
Hatfield, James to Nancy Broyles 5-1-1851
Hatfield, John to Elizabeth Hatfield 8-11-1840 (8-12-1840)
Hatfield, Samuel to Sarah Davis 3-25-1877
Hatmaker, Aaron T. to Jane Miller 5-9-1859 (5-10-1859)
Hatmaker, Aaron to Mary A. German 1-25-1862 (1-26-1862)
Hatmaker, Aaron to Nancy Bullock 5-27-1869
Hatmaker, Calvin to Elizabeth Ann Bullock 11-23-1872 (11-24?-1872)
Hatmaker, Cornelius to Elizabeth Sharp 7-27-1858 (7-28-1858)
Hatmaker, Daniel to Nancy Low 10-2-1873 (10-3-1873)
Hatmaker, Danl. to Martha J. Harmon 8-18-1853
Hatmaker, Dunken to Peany Sharp 5-23-1863 (5-24-1863)
Hatmaker, G. Sr. to Lavina Germin 12-31-1864 (no return)
Hatmaker, Henderson to Louisa Jarman 6-2-1849
Hatmaker, Henry to Martha Jarman 7-30-1875
Hatmaker, Jacob to Delila Carver 3-14-1840 (3-15-1840)
Hatmaker, Jacob to Polly Hatmaker 11-8-1849 (11-9-1849)
Hatmaker, James F. to Mattie Carver 1-4-1873 (11-29-1873)
Hatmaker, James to Sarah Murray 1-26-1850 (1-27-1850)

Hatmaker, James to Sophia Cooper 3-14-1846
Hatmaker, Jno. B. to M. E. Harmon 7-15-1878 (8-23-1878)
Hatmaker, John to Caroline Sloven 9-25-1858
Hatmaker, John to Polina Sharp 9-8-1862 (9-9-1862)
Hatmaker, Jos. to M. J. Sharper 2-19-1877 (2-22-1877)
Hatmaker, Joseph to Millie Wallace 2-21-18877 (2-23-1877)
Hatmaker, Lacy to Barbara Cooper 12-20-1860 (12-23-1860)
Hatmaker, Lewis to Jane Maddern 12-31-1880
Hatmaker, Louisa to Martha Bailey 6-6-1874 (6-7-1874)
Hatmaker, Malikeer to Elizabeth Murray 2-24-1842 (2-27-1842)
Hatmaker, N. to Caty Richardson 3-4-1878 (3-6-18878)
Hatmaker, T. D. to M. C. Burton 7-17-1876 (11-12-1876)
Hatmaker, Thos. to Elisa Hatmaker 11-19-1875
Hatmaker, Wm. to Martha J. Queener 9-19-1855 (no return)
Hatmaker, Wm. to Susan Murray 9-15-1853 (no return)
Haun, Geo. W. to Flourance Dean 12-28-1869
Haun, M. D. to Juda Logan 8-23-1869
Hawkins, Columbus to Cinthia Massingal 12-23-1880 (12-25-1880)
Hawkins, Saml. to M. J. Huckabay 12-28-1877 (12-30-1877)
Hawkins, Samuel to Nancy Roach 11-8-1870
Hawkins, W. H. to Sarah Sharp 12-2-1863 (no return)
Haynes, William to Endry Hill 11-19-1855 (11-27-1855)
Hays, J. W. to Margret Perkins 11-11-1865
Hays, John to Lydia Sharp 9-8-1855 (9-13-1855)
Hayslip, David to Rachael Beams 10-15-1846
Hayslip, Henre to Martha Boulton 4-7-1850
Hayslip, Robert to Elizabeth Lay 12-25-1841
Heather, Anthony to Elizabeth Keller 5-24-1839 (5-26-1839)
Heatherley, Alvis to Tempy Lumpkins 2-3-1869
Heatherley, George to Damaris Siller 3-1-1864 (4-2-1865)
Heatherley, John J. to Eliza F. Gray 12-30-1872 (1-2-1873)
Heatherley, Wm. to Lydia Gray 11-22-1870 (11-27-1870)
Heatherly, A. to Sarah Ford 10-26-1846 (no return)
Heatherly, Andrew to Sarah Craig 3-2-1839 (no return)
Heatherly, G. W. to Sarah Brown 11-6-1880 (2-26-1881)
Heatherly, James to Susanah Wright 11-16-1874
Heatherly, Jas. Jr. to S. Wright 11-16-1874 (Nov. 1874)
Heatherly, John to Lucinda Cloud 4-4-1849 (no return)
Heatherly, Stephan to Elizabeth Riggs 9-6-1869 (9-9-1869)
Heatherly, Wm. to Nancy Lynch 4-8-1856 (4-10-1856)
Henager, Wm. W. to Lidda E. Childress 2-26-1862 (3-6-1862)
Henderson, William C. to Nancy Sanders 3-21-1838
Heninger, Hiram to A. C. Powers 7-15-1874 (7-17-1874)
Heninger, Patten to Sarah Heninger 3-3-1859 (3-4-1859)
Henry, Wm. to Malinda Hill 10-10-1874 (10-11-1874)

Henson, Tapley J. to Melinda McCarty 2-7-1843 (2-12-1843)
Heren, Prior to Liddy Parsons 4-25-1857 (4-26-1857)
Heron, Calaway to Mary Bratcher 2-6-1845 (2-9-1845)
Herrin, Armsted to Susan Lukes 2-13-1846 (2-15-1846)
Herrin, Pryor to Margaret Ponder 8-28-1841 (8-29-1841)
Herrin, Pryor to Margarett Pondon 8-28-1841 (8-29-1841)
Herring, S. E. to Delilah Moffort 5-31-1838 (6-10-1838)
Hester, Tho. D. to Leanna Smith 3-10-1860
Hetton, J. R. to M. L. Barton 3-11-1880
Heuson, Robert to Minerva Jones 11-24-1875
Hewitih, James to Elizabeth Anderson 8-30-1841 (no return)
Hicks, Edwin to Niche! Beams 1-18-1844
Hicks, John to Susan Reynolds 1-3-1877
Hicks, Thomas to Mary Thomson 6-3-1872 (6-5-1872)
Hicks, William B. to Mary Jane Perkins 3-9-1873
Hicks, Wm. Caswell to Racheal Douglass 11-16-1877
Higgins, James to Leny Turpine 8-26-1879
Higgs, Sandford to Pernelia Haley 11-25-1839 (11-28-1839)
Higgs, Westly to Polly Haley 8-30-1845
Hill, A. L. to Alice Smith 7-31-1880 (8-12-1880)
Hill, Clarvell to S. A. H. Walker 9-6-1852 (9-16-1852)
Hill, Dulin to Elizabeth Heatherly 7-16-1862 (7-17-1862)
Hill, Eli to Jane Johnson 6-28-1872 (6-29-1872)
Hill, Eligah to Marino Campbell 1-20-1863 (1-25-1863)
Hill, George to Nancy J. Sharp 2-9-1869
Hill, Hasel to Mary Jane Miller 1-24-1873 (1-30-1873)
Hill, Henry Jr. to Sarah Herrin 1-13-1848 (no return)
Hill, James H. to Sarah Harding 2-16-1872
Hill, John E. to S. C. Robison 5-30-1874 (5-31-1874)
Hill, John to Minerva J. Norton 6-25-1852
Hill, Kemuel to Nancy Williams 5-25-1875 (5-27-1875)
Hill, Kennel to Marida Glander 11-9-1850 (11-10-1850)
Hill, Lemuel to Frances Shelby 3-20-1856 (no return)
Hill, Lindsey to Nancy Sharp 12-8-1843 (1-10-1844)
Hill, Livel to Alcey Forester 11-14-1852 (11-18-1852)
Hill, Nathaniel to Mary Orick 1-5-1869 (1-7-1869)
Hill, Oliver to Ann Oakes 2-20-1839 (2-24-1839)
Hill, Peter to Martha Braden 9-15-1871 (9-21-1871)
Hill, Richard to Polly Ann Adkins 12-29-1879 (1-1-1880)
Hill, Robert to Sarah Smith 3-16-1857 (6-10-1858)
Hill, Sanford to R. E. Davis 11-21-1851 (11-27-1851)
Hill, Silvester to Minerva Tow 3-29-1859 (1859)
Hill, William to E. J. Sexton 10-4-1876 (10-8-1876)
Hilyard, Harison to Louisa Hutson 2-24-1863
Hinkle, Lewis to Elisabeth Jones 2-25-1879

Hinson, Jno. to Sarah Lovett 8-30-1843
Hise, Jesse to Mary Duncain 1-20-1838
Hitch, John to Hasy Sharp 1-18-1843 (1-22-1843)
Hix, John to Sarah Gayler 8-5-1868 (8-15-1868)
Hix, Nathaniel to Susanah Richman 11-26-1857
Hix, Wm. to Carline Thompson 12-8-1864 (no return)
Hobbs, Jeffrey R. to Nancy E. Cooper 6-13-1879
Hodges, Sampson to Permelia Ann Angel 12-16-1844
Hodges, Stephen to Jemimah Bryant 4-4-1875
Hoges, Sampson to Minerva Smith 9-28-1859
Holden, Henderson to Rebecca Adkins 11-2-1870
Holder, Thomas to Lucy Ann Riggs 2-19-1881 (2-20-1881)
Hollin, G. W. to Susan Bennett 8-7-1879
Hollingsworth, H. M. to Allice A. Marshall 9-15-1868 (9-16-1868)
Hollingsworth, J. C. to A. T. Bibee 1-21-1865 (no return)
Hollingsworth, Jas. M. to Jane Meador 6-6-1856 (6-7-1856)
Hollingsworth, John A. to Mary Hair 7-28-1863 (soh, no date)
Holloway, Joseph to Mary Helton 7-14-1853 (7-17-1853)
Holt, George to Elizabeth Fox 10-6-1853
Holt, James C. to Eady Tavy 4-7-1845
Holt, Noah to Milly Lawson 1-23-1854
Holt, Wilson to Mary Annaa Leach 4-22-1877
Honeycut, Hardy to Nancy Smith 2-10-1845 (2-13-1845)
Honeycutt, William to Louisa Smmiddy 7-30-1875 (8-1-1875)
Hood, John to Susan Miller 1-8-1865
Hope, Emily to Jas. Queener 4-14-1858
Hope, Jordan to Rody Douglass 5-19-1859
Hope, Ralph Izard to Lucinda J. Johnston 12-13-1848
Hope, Robt. R. to Martha Ann Izby? 8-25-1843 (8-27-1843)
Hopper, A. M. to Sarah Parker 3-1-1878
Hopper, Johnson to Sally Bridges 8-2-1855 (no return)
Housley, Crawford to Peny Ann Redenour 5-17-1879
Housley, Frank to Elizabeth Sparks 12-21-1868 (12-23-1868)
Housley, Franklin to Eliza Ann Smith 12-1-1871 (12-5-1871)
Housley, James to Catherine Heatherly 5-1-1865 (5-4-1865)
Housley, James to Cathrine Heatherly 5-1-1865 (no return)
Housley, John to Margaret Taylor 9-17-1856 (9-15?-1856)
Housley, Joseph to Martha Cates 2-6-1865
Housley, Pleasant to Beubeca Stouto 7-7-1876 (7-8-1876)
Housley, Pleasant to Martha Brown 2-28-1865 (3-2-1865)
Housley, Wm. to Sarah Comer 9-3-1856 (no return)
Hously, Crawford to Melinda Lett 9-3-1855 (9-6-1855)
Hously, Pleasant to Mary Dagly 12-16-1848 (no return)
Hubard, Calvin to Jane Reeves 9-23-1877
Hubbard, Andrew to Lewerety? Wildrige 8-19-1856 (8-29-1856)

Hubbard, Isaac to Elizabeth Phillip 4-12-1856
Hubbard, Jesse to Sarah Chavis 9-26-1839 (10-1-1839)
Hubbard, Marion to Mary Smith 8-31-1865 (9-1-1865)
Hubboard, Allen to Jane Chavis 9-16-1839
Hucheson, John to Martha Blevins 3-11-1864 (3-13-1864)
Huckaboy, Presley to Mary Bullock 5-2-1840 (5-3-1840)
Huckaby, Alf to Licey David 3-26-1857 (3-27-1857)
Huckaby, Armstrong to Mary J. Dial 11-28-1857 (11-29-1857)
Huckaby, C. to C. A. L. Grissell 3-19-1880 (3-28-1880)
Huckaby, Commodore to Serepta S. Adkins 12-22-1847
Huckaby, Elisha to Salitha Adkins 11-17-1847 (11-21-1847)
Huckaby, Haywood to Sarah Queener 4-17-1856
Huckaby, William to Nancy Millican 8-4-1839
Huckeby, Armstrong to Amanda Jane Turbinville 11-12-1873 (11-16-1873)
Huckeby, J. M. C. to Mary Angeline Boshears 11-24-1872
Huddleston, Jackson to Elizabeth Stanfill 2-21-1856
Huddleston, Rew to Nancy Stanfill 10-16-1864
Huddleston, Wm. to Hannah Gaylor 9-25-1853
Huddleston, Wm. to Jane Huddleston 1-13-1870 (3-14-1870)
Hudelson, Jackson to Mary Loe 9-14-1868
Hudelson, Marcilous to Elizabeth Bolen 6-13-1872
Hudelston, J. F. M. to Rachel Holt 12-24-1876
Hudelston, Wm. to Susanah Mink 2-13-1859
Huff, Jourdan to Patsy McKee 7-27-1853
Humphreys, H. to Melinda Weaver 12-11-1852 (12-12-1852)
Humphreys, Houston to Mahaly Boruff 9-8-1864 (no return)
Hundley, James to Nancy E. Thomas 3-8-1865 (3-9?-1865)
Hunley, James to Martha Emela Harding 5-17-1873 (5-18-1873)
Hunly, John to Angeletta Gross 10-24-1855 (10-25-1855)
Hunly, John to Martha Gross 7-21-1853 (7-21-1853)
Hunt, F. F. to Jane Adkins 1-30-1843 (sol, no date)
Hunter, Francis to Nicey Hatmaker 4-23-1864 (4-24-1864)
Hunter, Green C. to Eliza Douglass 2-12-1851 (4-7-1851)
Hunter, Henry to Martha Kineard? 1-21-1871 (1-22-1871)
Hunter, Henry to Susan Goin 9-7-1852 (9-9-1852)
Hunter, J. C. to Catherine Thomas 2-20-1879 (2-21-1879)
Hunter, J. H. to Ann Lumpkins 1-14-1874
Hunter, Jno. to Telitha Hart 10-3-1844 (10-6-1844)
Hunter, S. F. to Louisa Medlock 11-6-1874 (11-7-1874)
Hunter, Spencer to Lavina Jarman 11-24-1843 (no return)
Hunter, Squire to Frances Dabny 1-27-1847
Huntsinger, Noah to Nancy Branam 5-8-1873
Huthen?, Isaac to Mary Ann Carroll 11-25-1843 (no return)
Hutson, Anthony to Eliza Thomas 10-8-1859 (10-13-1859)

Hutson, Anthony to Elizabeth Bowling 12-23-1841 (12-26-1841)
Hutson, David to Rebecca Outen 4-14-18587 (4-16-1857)
Hutson, Elijah H. to Martha Robins 12-23-1879 (12-25-1879)
Hutson, George to July A. Claxton 3-8-1864
Hutson, Isaac G. to Mary Jane Sharp 12-16-1874 (12-17-1874)
Hutson, Isaac to Polly Ford 7-4-1842
Hutson, Isaac to Vira Jackson 10-2-1849
Hutson, James to Isabella Gray 6-17-1840 (no return)
Hutson, John H. to Mary E. Morrow 4-30-1865 (4-?-1865)
Hutson, John to Emily Pebly 11-14-1864 (11-23-1864)
Hutson, John to Nancey Sweat 1-6-1842 (no return)
Hutson, John to Reuhama Johnson 10-21-1848 (10-26-1848)
Hutson, Ruben to Emily J. Rains 1-20-1861
Hutson, Ruben to Martha McNew 5-30-1864 (5-31-1864)
Hutson, Thos. W. to Parley S. Sharp 11-1-1876 (11-2-1876)
Hutson, William to Celia Miller 4-6-1855 (4-8-1855)
Hutson, William to Tempy Pebly 2-7-1853 (2-5-1853)(sic)
Hyatt, E. J. to Lizy Bird 1-29-1865
Ingram, Levi to Nancy Morgana 3-28-1841
Ingram, Silas to Sarah Hampton 10-4-1843 (10-5-1843)
Ingram, William to Elizabeth Burriss 1-15-1849 (1-18-1849)
Ingram, Wm. to Nancy Dowell 3-31-1855 (8-8-1855)
Irvin, Jas. P. to Nancy Y. Kincaid 3-24-1845
Irvin, Robert to Sarah Smith 12-29-1846
Irwin, Jacob to Nancy Dossett 12-11-1871 (12-14-1871)
Irwin, M. F. to Minerva McNew 7-13-1863
Irwin, Nathaniel to Ann Myers 1-2-1869 (1-3-1869)
Irwin, Nathaniel to Elizabeth Rice 5-7-1863 (no return)
Irwin, Rufus to Patsy Lynch 10-28-1871 (11-2-1871)
Irwine, Walford to Surilda Brock 8-12-1874 (8-16-1874)
Isaac, Jarman to Thursey Ann Johnson 4-26-1873 (4-27-1873)
Ivey, A. P. to Sarah Kelso 2-24-1876
Ivey, Elisha to Olley Ivey 3-28-1881 (4-3-1881)
Ivey, Hogan to Josephine Ivey 3-7-1880 (3-19-1880)
Ivey, James to Elizabeth Ivey 12-4-1872 (12-7-1872)
Ivey, Joseph to Elizabeth Hubbard 8-19-1869 (8-20-1869)
Ivey, Wm. H. to M. J. Wiloughby 8-23-1879 (8-24-1879)
Ivey, Wm. to Cyntha Brock 8-17-1871
Ivey, Win, to Margaret Sheley 12-31-1857
Ivy, Amos to Eliza Ivy 9-1-1853 (9-3-1853)
Ivy, Ashley to E. McCully 8-3-1855 (no return)
Ivy, Ashly to Barbara Parker 6-9-1877 (6-10-1876?)
Ivy, Samuel H. to Mary Mcully 1-27-1857 (2-15-1857)
Izley, Lafayette to Martha T. Hope 10-19-1853 (8-8-1955?)
Jackson, Andrew to Katherine Loy 11-4-1838

Jackson, David to Mary Tuttle 3-5-1855 (3-8-1855)
Jackson, Dudley to Mandy Murray 6-10-1857
Jackson, Henry L. to Mary B. Thompson 1-10-1851
Jackson, Jacob to Martha Ford 5-16-1849
Jackson, James to Mahaly Wilson 1-16-1849 (no return)
Jackson, John N. to Susan A. Elkins 10-28-1847
Jackson, Kincaid to Mariah Sweat 4-9-1877 (4-10-1877)
Jackson, Linsay? to Anna Hatfield 4-2-1849 (4-4-1849)
Jackson, N. G. to Sarah Lambert 11-24-1864 (no return)
Jackson, William to Mahala Cooper 4-25-1840 (4-26-1840)
Jarman, John to Eleanor Brown 7-24-1847 (exe., no date)
Jarmon, John to E. J. Hatmaker 5-19-1880
Jennings, John to Julia Forrester 2-5-1880
Johnson, Ambrose O. to Rebecca Boulton 10-22-1865
Johnson, Andrew to Susan Elkins 8-30-1878 (9-1-1878)
Johnson, B. N. to S. C. Sumers 7-2-1866 (7-12-1866)
Johnson, Charles M. to Nancy Craig 3-6-1843 (no return)
Johnson, F. L. to Mary Keen 6-10-1854
Johnson, George W. to Sarah J. Madden 1-4-1849 (no return)
Johnson, H. S. to Julia Quener 11-21-1878
Johnson, Hiram to Mary Cox 3-10-1854
Johnson, J. F. to Levina Hill 12-13-1871 (12-14-1871)
Johnson, J. N. to Matilda Stout 7-31-1875
Johnson, James L. to Levina E. Johnson 7-27-1868 (7-30-1868)
Johnson, James to Lucinda Carnutt 12-17-1844 (no return)
Johnson, James to Lucy Archer 9-2-1869
Johnson, James to Mary E. Jordan 11-8-1864 (11-29-1864)
Johnson, Jas. to Eliza Adkins 2-4-1843 (2-5-1843)
Johnson, John W. to Julia Hunter 2-1-1879 (2-4-1879)
Johnson, Leonard to Elizabeth Johnson 12-23-1872 (12-26-1872)
Johnson, Louis J. to Caroline Housley 10-11-1849 (10-18-1849)
Johnson, Nathaniel to Elizabeth Hudleston 11-28-1860
Johnson, Pleasant to Coly Kirk 9-3-1853 (9-4-1853)
Johnson, R. M. to N. M. Jourdan 6-22-1863 (7-12-1863)
Johnson, Samuel L. to Dealpha Hill 11-23-1872 (11-24-1872)
Johnson, Sol. to Nancy Brumet 2-19-1858 (2-21-1858)
Johnson, Thomas to Sarah Ann Elkins 9-12-1879 (9-13-1879)
Johnson, W. to Lucinda Bowlinger 5-25-1868 (5-28-1868)
Johnson, Wm. to Dosee Adkins 3-25-1843 (3-26-1843)
Johnson, Wm. to Elizabeth Day 9-30-1861 (no return)
Johnson, Wm. to Jane Shelton 9-4-1879 (9-7-1879)
Jones, Calvin S. to Sarah Sharp 7-17-1861
Jones, Elbert to Patsey Parker 10-24-1880
Jones, Elisha to Celia Ann Ellison 2-1-1874
Jones, Ephraighn to Elizabeth Tye 12-11-1856

Jones, Ephraim to Easter R. Litton 8-26-1880
Jones, Isaac to Jane Romines 7-29-1859
Jones, Isaac to Mary Patterson 11-18-1856
Jones, J. C. to L. B. Ellison 4-11-1880
Jones, J. L. to Sarah Williamson 1-14-1854 (1-15-1854)
Jones, J. N. to Elizabeth Baily 7-14-1855 (no return)
Jones, J. W. to Elizabeth Faulkner 6-7-1880
Jones, James to Amelia J. Bryant 8-24-1875 (8-26-1875)
Jones, Jesse to Delany Harp 7-6-1848 (no return)
Jones, John to Elizabeth Evans 8-12-1874 (8-13-1874)
Jones, John to Sarah Powers 2-19-1845
Jones, L. D. to Kissiah Perkins 8-15-1878
Jones, Lewis F. to Cintey Lett 9-4-1858 (9-5-1858)
Jones, Pleasant W. to Ester Nickleson 2-27-1845
Jones, Pressly to Zephry Rose 8-17-1848 (8-7?-1848)
Jones, R. to Mary Peirce 2-15-1869 (2-25-1869)
Jones, Thomas to Nancy Sweat 5-22-1853 (5-25-1853)
Jones, Thos. A. to Sarah E. Walton 5-25-1871 (6-4-1871)
Jones, William to Susanah Richardson 10-23-1860 (10-26-1860)
Jones, Willy to Delilah Jones 8-25-1853
Jordan, John C. to Elizabeth Johnson 3-28-1874 (3-29-1874)
Jordan, John to Elizabeth Hudson 2-17-1855 (2-20-1855)
Jordan, Wm. to Rebecca Lawson 8-4-1859 (8-7-1859)
Joslin, Jas. W. to L. J. Kennedy 12-8-1854 (12-5?-1854)
Jourdan, John to Malinda Jones 4-11-1880
Jourdan, Robert W. to Louisa Virginia Nance 8-14-1849 (no return)
Keath, Gabriel to Duosy Puteet 8-15-1838 (8-19-1838)
Keeney, Joseph to Lavina Huff 7-14-1842
Keeney, Wm. M. to A. D. Hall 12-27-1870
Keenon, Thomas to Martha Puckett 12-30-1871
Keeny, Jackson to Cynthia A. Huff 10-12-1848 (10-14-1848)
Keeny, John L. to Minerva J. Walker 2-6-1848
Keith, William to Sally McGhee 1-26-1855 (1-27-1855)
Kelsoe, J. W. to Sarah Jones 5-6-1845 (5-27-1845)
Kenaday, Matt to Laphaney Marlon 11-17-1862 (11-27-1862)
Kenaday, Raus to Giney Burge 12-2-1865 (no return)
Kerr, John W. to Lucinda Siler 8-23-1871
Kerr, John to Mary Rains 10-31-1869
Kesefang, Wm. to China Rector 1-4-1878 (1-6-1878)
Kesterson, Frederick to Anna Lovely 11-28-1849 (no return)
Kesterson, H. C. to M. J. Smiddy 6-12-1880 (6-13-1880)
Kesterson, James to Clarinda Wheeler 7-10-1869 (7-11-1869)
Kesterson, James to Margarett Lovedy 1-13-1841 (1-14-1841)
Kesterson, John to Sarah Sweaton 7-31-1864
Kilbourn, E. C. to Elizabeth Miller 8-24-1851 (8-28-1851)

Kilby, Wm. C. to Mary Chadwell 7-10-1872 (7-31-1872)
Killer, John to Emiley Jones 5-25-1839 (no return)
Killion, Alexander to Sarah Cagle 10-23-1870
Kimberly, John Wesley to Eliz. Shepherd 1-30-1875 (1-31-1875)
Kincaid, Alexander to Mary Elizabeth Kincaid 11-25-1871 (11-26-1871)
Kincaid, Frank to Susan Fortner 9-23-1875 (9-25-1875) [B]
Kincaid, Franklin to Ann Cain 8-28-1843 (8-31-1843)
Kincaid, Harve to Brilly Myers 12-1-1875 (12-2-1875)
Kincaid, Harry C. to Mary J. Word 3-22-1847 (4-1-1847)
Kincaid, Isaac to Mahala Smith 1-6-1879 (1-9-1879)
Kincaid, James to Elizabethe Ivey 5-24-1871 (5-25-1871)
Kincaid, James to Mary Myers 1-27-1870
Kincaid, Jas. H. to Louisa J. Walker 8-9-1856 (8-14-1856)
Kincaid, John to Judia Wood 10-25-1852 (11-2-1852)
Kincaid, Lewis to Mary Rodgers 2-7-1880 (2-27-1880)
Kincaid, Lewis to Mary Rogers 2-7-1880 (2-27-1880)
Kincaid, M. M. to Martha J. Mars 8-30-1859 (9-6-1859)
Kincaid, Madison to Sarah E. Myers 11-24-1869 (11-24-1870?)
Kincaid, Peter to Mary Jane Sylivan 4-23-1874
Kincaid, Robert to Pricillia Kincaid 4-29-1874 (4-30-1874)
Kincaid, S. C. to M. E. Myres 11-22-1876 (11-23-1876)
Kincaid, Sip to Malisa Hale 6-2-1879
King, David to Louisa Siller 2-9-1865
King, David to Oma Pennington 3-5-1865
King, Enos to Nancey Angel 8-29-1839
King, Geo. W. to Nancy Morgan 11-21-1875
King, Harvey to Holly Morgan 11-25-1875
King, Jackson H. to Eliza Angel 4-24-1842
King, Leander to Polley Smith 7-20-1842 (7-21-1842)
King, T. M. C. to Emely Teagle 6-5-1865 (6-8-1865)
King, Wm. to Martha Richardson 8-21-1843 (8-22-1843)
Kirby, John to Eliza Massengil 11-5-1870 (12-8-1870)
Kirk, William C. to Irena Miller 7-16-1841
Kirk, William to Eliza Fullington 2-3-1853 (2-4-1853)
Kirkpatrick, O. R. to H. Talley 9-18-1850
Kitt, James to Nancy Perkins 3-16-1873
Laide?, J. W. to Lucinda Sweatt 11-1-1870
Lamar, [sham to Rebecca McFarland 4-3-1849 (4-4-1849)
Lamar, William to Sarah Irvin 12-24-1861 (12-25-1862)
Lambden, C. G. to Elizabeth (Miss) Smiddy 2-27-1868
Lambden, James to Feba L. Hamblen 9-6-1879
Lambdin, E. J. to M. E. Leach 12-2-1880
Lambdin, E. J. to Martha Fox 1-10-1878
Landen, James W. to Selatha Siler 9-26-1874
Landon, Ivin to Mary L. Childers 12-13-1860 (12-20-1860)

Landrum, David to Martha J. Lovely 10-24-1876 (10-25-1876)
Landrum, Wm. K. to Louisa Lovely 5-2-1876 (5-11-1876)
Langley, Andrew to Mary Reynolds 2-12-1873 (2-20-1873)
Langley, Ephraam to Mary Murray 1-3-1841 (1-4-1841)
Langley, John to Elizabeth Smiddy 2-17-1851 (2-20-1851)
Larew, J. C. to Lizzie Wood 12-2-1880 (11?-2-1880)
Large, James J. to Mary (Miss) Claibourn 10-6-1868 (12?-20-1868)
Lassen, Andrew to Litha Rose 11-25-1858
Lawson, Hutson to Sarah Rose 9-22-1858
Laudermilk, Wm. Maney to Idea Morgan 1-20-1881
Lauson, Jas. F. to Martha Miller 12-22-1870
Law, Michael to Juda McGhee 2-3-1881
Law, Wm. to Sarah Rickett 7-16-1879
Laws, Joseph M. to Elizabeth Belelw 7-25-1842 (no return)
Lawson, Aaron to Tabitha Wilhite 1-20-1853 (no return)
Lawson, Absolam to Elizabeth Roler 10-10-1863 (10-16-1863)
Lawson, Andrew to Elizabeth Rose 1-21-1844
Lawson, Archabald to Cyntha Collins 7-7-1873 (7-10-1873)
Lawson, Carter to Nancy Thompson 8-20-1879 (8-23-1879)
Lawson, David to Ann Lawson 2-18-1842
Lawson, David to Nancy Rose 1-15-1880
Lawson, G. W. to Sarah S. McCullah 2-26-1881 (3-6-1881)
Lawson, George to Susannah Adkins 10-22-1848
Lawson, H. M. to M. Wilson 6-20-1878 (6-23-1878)
Lawson, Henry to Lucinda Bennet 12-15-1844
Lawson, Henry to Sarah Rose 9-27-1841
Lawson, Isom to Elizabeth Holt 11-5-1854
Lawson, J. C. to Sarah Lee 11-5-1879
Lawson, J. L. to Lean Davis 9-16-1880
Lawson, Jacob to Vicia Luallen 1-5-1844 (1-7-1844)
Lawson, James to Catherine Miller 12-16-1872
Lawson, John W. to Permelia Ann Perkins 9-22-1865
Lawson, Nathan to Nancy Perkins 12-4-1871
Lawson, Reece to Martha A. Settle 3-24-1872 (3-26-1872)
Lawson, Richard C. to Lucinda Slier 12-26-1840
Lawson, Robert to Nancy Stanfill 12-10-1861 (12-19-1861)
Lawson, W. F. to Martha Smith 11-30-1879
Lawson, William to Elizabeth Benet 8-19-1841
Lawson, Wm. to M. J. McKidy 7-1-1878
Lawson, Y. S. to T. L. Deatherage 7-7-1878
Laxton, Jesse to Jane Thompson 11-20-1849 (no return)
Lay, Calvin to Hanah Smith 3-19-1878 (3-28-1878)
Lay, Calvin to Nancy Baird 3-14-1876 (3-19-1876)
Lay, David to Tyrena Flatford 9-9-1847 (no return)
Lay, Elisha to Martha Williamson 3-2-1877 (3-4-1877)

Lay, Francis H. to Florence Ayers 3-14-1879 (3-20-1879)
Lay, Henderson to Serelda Heatherly 11-20-1862 (no return)
Lay, Hiram to Conny Lay 2-15-1849 (2-18-1849)
Lay, Isaac to Elizabeth Putteet 2-10-1856 (2-11-1856)
Lay, Isaac to Martha Dial 8-30-1850 (11-12-1850)
Lay, Isaac to Rachael Rogers 3-7-1852
Lay, Jackson to E. J. Merida 7-8-1877
Lay, James to Emily Bodkin 12-4-1856 (12-11-1856)
Lay, James to Emly Gibson 11-23-1865 (11-26-1865)
Lay, James to has Grant 10-17-1840 (no return)
Lay, James to Nancy Hamilton 12-26-1880
Lay, James to Rachel Baird 2-4-1875
Lay, James to Thirey Grant 9-27-1857
Lay, Jas. F. to Marda? Jane Eldretlh 8-18-1870
Lay, Jesse to Cawley Lay 12-8-1839
Lay, Jesse to Susan A. Brook 2-27-1876
Lay, Jessee to Pollyann Perkins 3-1-1863 (3-5-1863)
Lay, Jno. to Elizabeth Murray 11-30-1843
Lay, John D. to America Brown 9-18-1871 (10-1-1871)
Lay, John D. to Ruminty Jane Creekmore 4-1-1869
Lay, John R. to Nancy K. Davis 10-5-1873
Lay, John to Cynthis Stanfill 4-7-1853
Lay, Lewis to Jane McCay 7-24-1878
Lay, Lewis to Mary Lay 8-12-1858
Lay, Lewis to Peggy Lawson 12-18-1864
Lay, Michael to Elizabeth Ralyaa 1-13-1859
Lay, Michael to Lydia Beard 9-20-1840
Lay, Moses to Delila Adkins 8-14-1839 (8-15-1839)
Lay, Moses to Mary Thompson 5-8-1856
Lay, Peter to Rebecca Croley 2-14-1856
Lay, Pryor to Rebecca Stanfill 11-3-1863 (11-8-1863)
Lay, Spencer to Cynthia Perkins 7-4-1880
Lay, Spencer to Martha Jane Baird 4-4-1863 (4-14-1863)
Lay, Thomas to Delila Croley 10-20-1849
Lay, Thomas to Drusy Adkins 8-21-1855 (8-23-1855)
Lay, Thomas to Sarah Morrow 7-16-1864 (7-17-1864)
Lay, William L. to Elizabeth Anderson 12-14-1872
Lay, William M. to Rachal Stanfill 6-19-1868 (6-21-1868)
Lay, William to Jane Puteet 9-21-1854 (9-28-1854)
lay, William to Nancy Croley 12-23-1848
Lay, William to Sarah Douglass 6-4-1840
Lay, Wm. to Lucy A. Lay 7-25-1858
Leach, D. F. to Frances Nicholson 7-26-1849
Leach, John M. to Ageline Chapman 4-15-1841 (5-3-1841)
Leach, Josiah Jr. to Mary Holt 1-10-1879

Leach, Josiah to Lucy J. Broos 3-14-1850 (4-14-1850)
Leach, Preston to Theresy J. Hunter 4-2-1859 (4-3-1859)
Leach, Robinson to Freely Adkins 8-26-1851 (8-28-1851)
Leach, Russel to Anna Scritchfield 8-5-1851 (8-10-1851)
Leach, Russel to Mary Proffitt 4-22-1872 (4-23-1872)
Leach, Sneed to Jane Pope 1-2-1878
Leach, Wesly to Mahaly Smith 10-29-1853 (1-22-1854)
Leach, William to Angeline Paul 7-17-1875
Leach, Wm. to Angeline Paul 7-17-1875 (7-11?-1875)
Lee, Andrew to Eliza Taylor 1-28-1874
Lee, Andrew to Polley Taylor 7-16-1875
Leeper, Willis to Elisabeth Armstrong 2-16-1876 (2-17-1876)
Lett, Joseph to Sarah A. Miller 10-22-1864 (10-28-1864)
Lett, L. M. to Martha M. Woodson 2-8-1875 (2-11-1875)
Lett, Wm. to Hester A. Glenn 10-17-1863 (not returned)
Lewallen, Jasper to Mary Jane Delk 12-21-1873
Lewallen, John to Harriet Burrass 2-13-1862
Lewellen, John to Julia Parker 5-27-1879
Lewis, D. S. to Lizzie McNeely 11-15-1880 (11-27-1880)
Lewis, J. L. to T. M. Rogers 9-4-1872 (9-5-1872)
Like, Leavi to Martha Bryant 9-2-1864
Lindamood, B. W. to Nancy Lay 1-16-1878
Lindamood, Clarance R. to Malinda J. Lindamood 6-17-1872
(6-18-1872)
Lindsay, A. B. to Martha Lindsay 7-9-1847
Lindsay, A. W. to Ceila Purkapile 11-12-1879 (11-16-1879)
Lindsay, A. W. to Elisa J. Coker 3-23-1876 (3-25-1876)
Lindsay, Andrew to Kisiah Gray (no dates)
Lindsay, C. S. to Volly Bowling 9-16-1850 (9-17-1850)
Lindsay, C. to N. Lovley 1-22-1873
Lindsay, Cornelius to Nancy Lovely 1-22-1873 (1-23-1873)
Lindsay, J. T. to N. A. Hatmaker 1-3-1877 (1-4-1877)
Lindsay, Robert to M. E. Green 7-16-1840
Lindsay, Thomas to Emoria Adkins 2-15-1872
Lindsay, William to Huldah Cooper 8-9-1839 (8-14-1839)
Lindsay, William to Mary Ann Stoks 11-13-1868 (11-14-1868)
Lindsey, A. B. to Marthey Gross 7-8-1865 (7-12-1865)
Lindsey, A. W. to Martha Hutson 10-12-1865
Lindsey, Mathew to Sarah E. Dunken 3-30-1861
Lindsey, Wm. to Barbary Gayler 8-11-1858
Linhart, Charles H. to Elizabeth Sharp 10-9-1869 (10-14-1869)
Lister, Voluntine to Mary M. Malicote 10-18-1864 (10-20-1864)
Litre!, George to Emely Raines 12-17-1874
Little, Calvin to Nancy J. Jackson 11-10-1839
Little, J. B. to Olly M. Kincaid 9-26-1854 (9-27-1854)

Litton, Cornelius to Eliza Chittwood 2-30?-1840 (1-30-1849)
Litton, Oliver to Nelly Brown 1-10-1849
Loe, Fielding to Sarah Carrolle 1-12-1843
Lofty, Alexander to Metilda Prock 6-23-1842
Logan, Hiram to Mary Parker 10-19-1865
Logan, Hiram to Nerva Jane Logan 7-22-1880
Logan, J. B. to L J. Mackey 2-8-1880
Logan, James to Levina Woard 10-17-1841
Logan, John to Anna Benneett Adkins 1-24-1873
Logston, A. H. to Mary Johnson 12-22-1880
Logue, George to Caroline Buckhanan 3-1-1860
Longmire, Jas. O. to Manda Wilson 11-15-1865 (no return)
Longmire, John to Mary Mallicoat 10-12-1870 (10-13-1870)
Longmire, Marcellus to Leah Huff 12-25-1851
Longmire, William to Christina Wilson 3-27-1879
Longmire, William to Rebecca Graves 9-11-1849 (9-13-1849)
Lotz, Frederic to Eliza J. Trail 2-5-1861
Loveday, C. W. to F. M. Dabney 11-17-1869 (12-6-1869)
Lovell, Corcelious to Martha J. Stanafill 9-19-1875
Lovely, A. to Lucinda Murry 5-15-1877 (5-7?-1877)
Lovely, Caswell to Mary Jane Wood 1-1-1874 (1-4-1874)
Lovely, David to Margaret Lindsay 10-2-1872 (10-3-1872)
Lovely, Henry to Elizabeth Lovely 3-19-1872 (3-20-1872)
Lover, Balintine to Louisa Anderson 4-30-1843
Lovet, Moses to Rachel Rozier 10-15-1863 (10-23-1863)
Lovett, David to Matilda Bird 5-26-1841
Lovett, Jesse to Hester Thompson 8-2-1838
Lovett, Jesse to Nancy Dowell 12-29-1849 (exe.--no date)
Lovett, Jessee to Mary Woods 11-29-1865 (no return)
Lovett, Valentine R. to Nancy J. Moses 11-27-1862
Lovitt, Alexander to Elizabeth Trail 7-6-1854
Lovitt, John to Delana Harmo 9-4-1848 (9-5-1848)
Lovitt, Joshua to Lucinda Harmon 10-2-1854 (8-8?-1855)
Lovutt, Moses to Lulcinda Sutton 12-24-1872 (12-25-1872)
Low, Elias to Catherine Ayers 4-11-1875
Low, L. D. to H. Baily 8-23-1845 (no return)
Low, Riley to Emmaline Clark 8-15-1875
Loy, F. H. to Sarah Brown 10-12-1864 (no return)
Loy, Henderson to Sally Stout 3-17-1843 (no return)
Loy, Henderson to Sarelda Heatherly 5-1-1865 (5-4-1865)
Loyd, A. to Ann Williams 4-7-1877 (4-8-1877)
Loyd, Alexander to Lucinda McDonald 11-20-1841 (11-21-1841)
Loyd, Andrew to Mary Jeffers 4-16-1840
Luallen, Mathew to Susan Lawson 2-11-1841
Luits, John to Hester Ann Lay 1-16-1851 (no return)

Lumkins, Wm. to Jennie Boshears 10-9-1876
Lumpkins, Absolum to Mary Goin 10-15-1846 (10-18-1846)
Lumpkins, Daniel to Matilda Kay 12-12-1873 (12-14-1873)
Lumpkins, James to Margaret Pearce 12-27-1880 (12-28-1880)
Lumpkins, Janus to Susan Chavis 7-8-1840 (7-24-1840)
Lumpkins, Joseph to Phebe McCarty 3-20-1853
Lumpkins, Wm. to Anna Yount 7-13-1872
Lynch, A. J. to Anna Dunn 6-18-1880 (6-20-1880)
Lynch, Nilson to Sarah Dossett 3-19-1838 (3-21-1838)
Lynch, Sidney to Aoral Sequin 1-7-1847
Lynch, W. W. to Mary J. Pebly 7-9-1852 (7-18-1852)
Lynch, Wash to Tilda Nash 9-10-1880 (9-12-1880)
Mackeye, James to M. D. Case 6-5-1879
Mackin, Michael to Susan Collins 5-18-1850 (5-21-1850)
Mackin, Michael to Susan Collins 5-18-1850 (no return)
Maclon, Thomas to Peggy A. Wilson 6-2-1855 (6-10-1855)
Maddern, Wm. to Sarah Richardson 11-22-1879 (11-27-1879)
Madrin, Robt. to Tempy Cox 3-7-1855 (3-8-1855)
Mahan, M. E. to Jane Archer 9-13-1855
Mahan, Milton M. to Louisa Archer 9-16-1875
Mahon, Alfred to Sarah Siler 3-4-1852
Main, Benjamin to Susan Siller 8-27-1865
Main, John C. to Nancy Bird 7-24-1865
Maize, Rice to Elizabeth Ingle 5-17-1868
Malaby, William to Nancy Sanders 1-2-1849 (1-3-1849)
Malicoat, Alvis to M. U. Sutton 4-3-1880
Malicoat, Calvin to Anna Cox 4-23-1876
Malicoat, John to Elizabeth Bratcher 11-19-1870 (11-23-1870)
Malicoat, Milton to Martha Miller 4-18-1870
Malicote, Elbelrt to Lucinda Chapman 8-19-1876 (8-20-1877)
Malicote, Joel H. to Livinia Lynch 3-30-1875
Malicote, John to Nancy E. Taylor 2-8-1856 (no return)
Malicote, Mary M. to Voluntine Lister 10-22-1864 (10-28-1864)
Malicote, Wm. to Ceala A. Miller 12-14-1863 (12-17-1863)
Mallicoat, Georg W. to Parlena Lofty 12-24-1874
Mallicoat, Simeon to Nancy Wheeler 7-14-1854 (no return)
Mallicoat, Simeon to Sarah Reed 2-5-1850 (4-1-1850)
Manuel, A. to Emeline Gearman 6-15-1877
Maples, J. S. to Permelia A. Hall 10-3-1878
Marcum, Arthur to Nancy Delk 3-6-1843 (3-7-1843)
Marcum, G. W. to Mary Anna Frank 4-3-1843 (5-5-1843)
Marcum, Wm. C. to Cyntha Gentry 5-4-1846 (1-26-1848)
Marcurum, Calvin to Margaret Claxton 6-18-1868 (6-19-1868)
Marcurum, Gilbert to Malissa Childress 12-15-1873 (12-18-1873)
Marler, George to Mary J. Hamptoon 9-8-1846

Marler, Paul to Sarah G. Wilson 2-7-1870 (2-20-1870)
Marlin, Charles G. to Elizabeth Runnels 3-27-1838
Mario, Manuel to Martha Stowers 4-24-1853
Marlow, Alexander to Surilda Wilson 11-2-1874 (11-15-1874)
Marlow, Calvin to Isey McGee 11-14-1878 (11-17-1878)
Marlow, Finly to Nancy Sharp 2-27-1847
Marlow, Reuben to Anna Ervin 9-26-1850
Marlow, Thos. to M. A. Wilson 11-9-1860 (11-11-1860)
Marlow, William to Elisabeth Kenady 4-6-1876 (4-13-1876)
Marlow, William to Elizabeth Kenedy 2-26-1877
Marlow, Wm. to Clara Phillips 11-2-1878
Marshal, James M. to Elizabeth Smith 10-14-1844 (10-17-1844)
Marshall, Eugene to Louiza McAmis 9-19-1870 (9-20-1870)
Martin, Hener to Sarena Helton 4-9-1857
Martin, James to Mahala Longmire 2-26-1842 (no return)
Martin, John to Mary Helton 9-22-1855
Martin, Sampson to Ann Roker 8-1-1839 (8-4-1839)
Martin, Susan to Joseph A. Pilkington 4-20-1843
Masengill, Jas. W. to Mary Tuttle 12-31-1869 (1-22-1870)
Massengill, John R. to Rebecca Lawson 12-29-1870 (no return)
Massingale, Matthew to Margaret Miller 10-6-1853
Massingill, Henry C. to Mary Day 4-27-1876
Massingill, Jas. W. to Mary Tuttle 12-31-1869 (1-1-1870)
Massingill, Jordana to Sarah Carroll 5-25-1869 (5-27-1869)
Matlock, John to Sarah Miles 1-4-1871
Maupiin, Willialm to Elizabeth Childress 10-8-1874 (10-10-1874)
Maupin, Amos to H. Hollingsworth 11-1-1853 (10?-?-1853)
Maupin, Henry to Hester Ann Cain 8-20-1847 (8-25-1847)
Maupin, James to Sally Pebly 1-30-1855 (2-8-1855)
Maupin, John B. to Armena E. Ivey 12-3-1879
Maupin, L. to M. W. Hollingsworth 5-16-1855 (5-17-1855)
Mayatt, Peter to Mary Grant 4-7-1871 (4-14-1871)
Mayatt, Peter to Mary Wilson 9-13-1864 (9-15-1864)
Mayatt, Peter to Mary Wilson 9-13-1864 (no return)
Mayres, Wm. H. to Sarah J. Bratcher 12-25-1854 (12-28-1854)
Mays, Giller to Elisabeth Jane Croley 4-17-1865
Mays, John to Juda Rickett 2-29-1880
Mays, Ralph to Susan Mays 6-15-1847
Mays, William L. to Elizabeth Golden 10-18-1872
Maze, Wm. D. to Sarah Reagan 10-8-1851
Mazingo, Benj. F. to Margaret Queener 8-8-1872
Mazingo, Fielding to Emely Smith 1-20-1870 (1-23-1870)
McAmis, D. C. to Mary Ann Marshall 3-22-1870
McCall, George to Elizabeth Gatlin 1-12-1851
McCamey, James to Nancy J. Willson 10-27-1857 (10-25?-1857)

McCarmic, Jno. to Bettie Tramel 3-24-1877 (3-25-1877)
McCarter, Thomas to M. J. Fullington 6-2-1851 (6-3-1851)
McCarty, Daniel to Sarah Sweat 10-16-1847 (10-17-1847)
McCarty, J. L. to E. E. Wells 12-13-1875 (12-16-1875)
McCarty, John W. to Nancy Davis 5-6-1871
McCarty, John Wesley to Mary Jane Lynch 10-11-1872 (10-17-1872)
McClain, John to Hester Ann Muzingo 12-18-1864 (12-22-1864)
McClain, William to M. J. Pierce 4-7-1856 (4-10-1856)
McClary, F. B. to Julia Woodson 12-24-1878 (12-25-1878)
McClary, Preston to Eliza Brassfield 1-29-1840 (no return)
McClary, William to Nancey McGlothlin 8-5-1840 (9-8-1840)
McClelin, Jeremiah to Susan Smith 8-22-1872
McCollock, James A. to Nancy Suter 10-15-1843
McCovy, Sterling to Juda Evans 9-26-1878
McCoy, Andrew E. to Mary Gibson 7-7-1854 (7-16-1854)
McCoy, Jos. to Salina Adkins 7-5-1862 (7-6-1862)
McCoy, Stephen to Anjaline Hamling 5-2-1875
McCullah, J. A. to Elizabeth Greekmore 10-6-1859
McCullah, James A. to Mary Williams 2-26-1854
McCully, Harvey to Rhoda Davison 11-17-1877 (11-18-1877)
McCully, James to Eliza Right 8-18-1850 (no return)
McCully, James to Mary J. Miller 8-18-1865 (8-20-1865)
McCully, Job to Patsy Ivy 8-19-1853 (8-21-1853)
McCully, John to Nancy Dossett 11-30-1878
McCully, Wm. to Elizabeth Smith 2-23-1866 (2-25-1866)
McDonald, James to Melind Lawson 5-1-1844 (5-2-1844)
McDonald, Samuel to Rebecca Reed 12-28-1846 (1-14-1847)
McDonold, Alleln to Christena Lauson 12-25-1849
McElkins, Minatt to Martha Jane Violett 1-20-1872
McElkins, Mynatt to Mornun Murray 3-9-1846
McFarland, Arthur to Winy Geesly 11-25-1853 (11-27-1853)
McFarland, Frank to M. J. Hubbard 2-15-1875 (2-16-1875)
McFarland, Jas. G. to Matilda E. Dougger 4-12-1858
McFarland, John J. to Eliza Cox 6-8-1868
McFarland, Tho. to Matilda Oatan 2-2-1857 (2-6-1857)
McFarland, Thomas to Josephine Ellison 1-24-1871
McFarlin, Franklin to M. J. Hubbard 2-15-1875
McFarlin, Thos. to Angeline Wyrick 1-28-1879 (1-30-1879)
McGee, Alexander to Louisa Carroll 9-14-1875 (9-19-1875)
McGee, James to Polly Patterson 1-8-1848 (1-10-1848)
McGee, John W. to Hannah Phillips 12-24-1879
McGee, John to Hanah Marlow 12-31-1868 (3-27-1869)
McGee, Wm. to H. J. Worley 3-17-1879 (3-21-1879)
McGhee, Calvin to Angeline Patterson 10-1-1879 (1-5-1879)
McGlauthlin, Chas. to Manda M. Butler 12-26-1855 (1-3-1856)

McGlothlin, Jas. to Roda Gossage 10-24-1876 (10-30-1876)
McGoin, ---- to Cola Kirk 3-22-1850 (3-24-1850)
McGran, Wm. to Martha McCully 10-1859 (11-11-1859)
McGraw, Frank to Polly Pierce 6-16-1874 (6-20-1874)
McGraw, John to Jane Pierce 12-17-1865 (no return)
McGraw, John to Susan Smith 5-7-1855
McHone, Andrew to Eliza Jackson 8-8-1844
McKee, Alfred to Mary Hill 8-31-1853 (no return)
McKee, Robt. to Polly Ann Owen 5-15-1856
McKeehan, James to Obediance Richardson 9-14-1849 (9-16-1849)
McKeehan, John to Mary Sutherland 8-30-1853 (9-1-1853)
McKeehan, Wm. J. to Susan Richardson 11-24-1860 (11-25-1860)
McKenney, Shadrack J. to Vasta J. Carr 12-1-1864
McNeal, M. M. to L. V. Claiborn 1-16-1874 (1-18-1874)
McNeeley, James to Nancy Curnutt 11-8-1872 (11-10-1872)
McNeeley, Rufus to Mary Madron 11-22-1871 (11-232-1871
McNeeley, Wm. to Nancy Jane Spangler 9-4-1871 (9-6-1871)
McNeely, Godfrey to Matilda A. Kimberling 6-13-1865
McNeely, Jno. C. to Evaline Spangler 7-22-1876 (7-23-1876)
McNeely, John to Martha Goin 11-24-1852 (11-25-1852)
McNeely, Wm. H. to Anna Carroll 7-3-1855
McNew, Elisha to Mary E. Rogers 11-16-1868 (11-19-1868)
McNew, F. P. to Sally Maupin 10-25-1844 (10-29-1844)
McNew, James H. to Olivia E. Kecaide 11-23-1868 (11-25-1868)
McNew, John to Elizabeth McGlathlin 4-7-1852
McNew, Tho. to Louisa Overbey 8-11-1859
McNiel, John to Margaret Miller 9-2-1873 (9-4-1873)
McVay, J. C. to Amelia J. Vaughn 1-5-1881
McVey, William M. to Louiza N. Smith 8-18-1873
Meaders, James to Frances Kreckmore 5-13-1838
Meaders, Jeremiah to Mary Crickmore 3-11-1839 (10th day 1840)
Meaders, Joseph to Cintha Crickmon 7-26-1840
Meador, J. M. to M. A. Angel 12-23-1877
Meador, Thos. W. to Mary Chapmana 3-5-1873 (3-6-1873)
Meador, W. J. to Hellen J. Sargent 10-10-1870 (10-27-1870)
Meadors, George B. to Lucinda Moore 10-3-1848
Meadors, Joseph to Raganer Stephans 2-6-1873
Meadors, It F. to H. A. Brown 12-7-1855 (12-9-1855)
Meadows, Edward to Ann Neal 7-26-1854
Medlock, M. D. to Mace Golden 8-24-1878
Medors, Job to Ormela Lovett 4-19-1879 (4-20-1879)
Meltibarger, Elijah to Mary A. Cambell 12-6-1864 (12-11-1864)
Melton, Alfred to Martha Lett 11-4-1859 (11-6-1859)
Melton, Alvis to Louis Lett 9-5-1862 (no return)
Melton, William to E. J. Ridenour 7-30-1853 (no return)

Melton, William to Elizabeth Ridenour 7-30-1853 (7-31-1853)
Mercurum, Calvin to Margaret Claxton 6-18-1868 (6-19-1868)
Merida, Jas. to S. Hicks 4-1-1878 (4-7-1878)
Meriday, Arch. to Sarah Paulson 8-6-1844 (8-7-1844)
Meriday, John to Sousan Johnson 11-10-1863
Merrida, John to Rebecca Stanfill 1-3-1873 (1-9-18873)
Mesgingor, Phillips to Levina McCarty 7-18-1839 (7-22-1839)
Miler, Henry to Mary McLane 4-5-1881
Miles, John W. to Elizabeth Lawson 5-12-1858
Miles, John W. to Levesta Wish 7-4-1880
Miles, N. L. to N. B. Shelton 2-25-1878
Miles, Samuel L. to Sabry Creekmore 5-15-1859
Miller, A. T.? to Sarah Ann Wiley 9-27-1838 (10-4-1838)
Miller, A. to Elizabeth Graves 8-10-1843 (8-13-1843)
Miller, Abraham to Annah McNew 9-23-1880
Miller, Alexander to Emely Huckaby 11-28-1868 (11-29-1868)
Miller, Andrew to Sarah McCulley 7-1-1839 (7-7-1839)
Miller, Ayres to Alice Miller 7-7-1880 (7-11-1880)
Miller, C. F. to Mary Welch 8-4-1875 (8-5-1875)
Miller, Daniel to Diana Brown 10-15-1848
Miller, David to M. J. Pennington 9-21-1878
Miller, Elias to Sarah Gray 1-26-1839 (1-27-1839)
Miller, Esau to Sarah Woods 1-29-1853 (1-30-1853)
Miller, Franklin to Barbary Longmire 12-18-1849 (12-25-1849)
Miller, Franklin to Polley Paulson 3-30-1842 (4-12-1842)
Miller, Franklin to Temperance Heatherley 11-26-1869 (11-28-1869)
Miller, G. W. to Elizabeth Vinsant 1-3-1880 (1-4-1880)
Miller, George W. to Mary Reede 10-22-1869 (10-23-1870)
Miller, George W. to Sarah Hutson 1-19-1861 (1-20-1861)
Miller, H. G. to Mary Bridges 9-8-18487 (9-16-1847)
Miller, Henry to Anna Parker 3-17-1879
Miller, Henry to Josephine Keeney 11-2-1870 (11-6-1870)
Miller, Isaac to Nancy Soaps 5-7-1846 (5-2-1847)
Miller, Jackson to Patsey Dossett 3-30-1842 (4-3-1842)
Miller, James M. to Mary Ford 1-14-1874 (1-18-1874)
Miller, James to Ann Sharp 11-18-1850 (11-21-1850)
Miller, James to Mary Crosswhite 6-12-1839 (no return)
Miller, James to Mattie Turner 9-12-1880
Miller, James to Nancy Davis 8-15-1853 (8-16-1853)
Miller, James to Nancy McCully 4-22-1843 (4-23-1843)
Miller, James to Rebecca Vinsant 9-18-1880 (9-19-1880)
Miller, James to Tobithy Bowline 1-2-1879
Miller, John H. to Frances M. Shepherd 10-11-1870 (10-16-1870)
Miller, John M. to Louisa Madren 2-25-1859
Miller, John to Jane Bunch 1-25-1881 (1-27-1881)

Miller, John to Lucretia Philllips 3-29-1873
Miller, John to Manda Yount 7-14-1874
Miller, John to Mary Jane Goin 12-19-1873 (12-20-1873)
Miller, Lemuel to Louisa Smith 3-1-1879
Miller, Lewis to Martha Williams 4-15-1860 (4-18-1860)
Miller, Lewis to Mary Elizabeth Miller 8-7-1871 (8-17-1871)
Miller, Mark to Catherine Baker 6-3-1871 (6-4-1871)
Miller, Martin to M. J. Kincaid 1-20-1879
Miller, Mike to Sarah C. Sumers 3-3-1876
Miller, Noah to Lidia Sharp 6-20-1874 (6-26-1874)
Miller, Peyton to Nancy Chapman 8-16-1851 (8-17-1851)
Miller, Pleasant to Martha Newman 2-4-1861 (2-7-1861)
Miller, Reubin to Fillis Miller 1-28-1869 (2-11-1869)
Miller, Robert to Matilda J. Lee 10-17-1864 (no return)
Miller, Robert to Selina Huckeby 1-9-1875 (1-10-1875)
Miller, Russell to Obedience Woodson 7-23-1880 (7-25-1880)
Miller, Sterling to Manda Adkins 5-3-1871 (5-4-1871)
Miller, Thomas to Margarett Loops 3-1-1842 (3-6-1842)
Miller, Washington to Amanda McCully 9-16-1874 (9-18-1874)
Miller, Wm. D. to Elisabeth Thompson 3-17-1876
Miller, Wm. G. to Luviney Nunn 8-31-1877
Miller, Wm. H. to Minerva Bruce 9-7-1856
Miller, Wm. to Catherine Curnutt 9-29-1869 (9-30-1869)
Milliner, D. G. H. to Emily Queener 11-6-1860
Mires, David to Elizabeth Hubbard 2-6-1857
Mitchell, L. F. to K. Walkup 11-17-1855
Mize, John M. to Mary F. Bustle 7-6-1858
Mobley, Archibald to Vicey Young 3-1-1840
Mobley, Levi to Susaner Williams 10-31-1877
Mondday, Saml. C. to Mary E. Turner 12-4-1870 (1-12-1871)
Monroe, S. E. to Lucinda Williams 1-31-1877
Montgomer, A. N. to Emma J. Clibourn 11-19-1870 (11-20-1870)
Moor, David to Rachael Fox 6-4-1856
Moore, B. C. to Susan Turner 1-29-1881 (1-30-1881)
Moore, James W. to Mary Hall 11-23-1843
Moore, William to Avy Shelton 4-30-1849 (5-1-1849)
Moore, Wm. Ephrim to Susan Davis 12-17-1841
Moore, Wm. J. to Matilda William 9-25-1860
Moore, Wm. to Anna J. Turner 10-11-1878 (10-13-1878)
More, Caleb to Mary F. Cox 10-8-1874
Morgan, Daniel to Malinda Whitaker 9-28-1851
Morgan, Ephram to Nancy Douglass 4-27-1865
Morgan, George to Louisa Hoper 3-9-1852 (3-11-1852)
Morgan, H. L. to S. J. Bennett 8-24-1879
Morgan, Wm. H. to Pricey A. Cain 10-29-1868

Morgan, Wm. to Susannah King 5-17-1846
Morton, James to Mahaley Longmire 2-26-1842 (no return)
Morton, Jas. to Anna Martha Meadow 5-29-1854 (6-?-1854)
Moser, G. W. to Lucy O. Owens 10-9-1876 (10-10-1876)
Moser, James A. to July Ann Moser 3-21-1881
Moses, Andrew to Dolaphana? Davis 12-18-1880
Moses, Elias to Nancy A. Anderson 1-26-1873
Moses, F. D. to Cotney Lovet 11-26-1863 (no return)
Moses, Holly D. to Mary Smithi 8-18-1879
Moses, Holly D. to S. Malissa Caudle 6-27-1844
Moses, Joshua to Sarah Creekmore 12-2-1842
Moses, Pleasant to Cathrine Lovet 4-12-1865
Mosier, Jacob to Eliza Hatmaker 12-23-1853 (no return)
Mosier, John to Mary Murray 3-1-1839 (3-6-1839)
Mosis, Francis to Sinthey Baird 4-20-1877
Mosley, John to Mahala Parton 11-5-1879
Mowell, Benjamin F. to Eliza Jackson 6-11-1857 (6-12-1857)
Moyres, John to Martha Miller 9-24-1853 (Sept 1853)
Mozier, George to Barbary Bullock 12-4-1854 (12-7-1854)
Mozier, Jacob to Eliza Hatmaker 12-23-1852
Mozier, Nathan to Polly Albright 12-2-1847 (no return)
Mozingo, Marshall to Jane Robins 10-11-1880
Mullins, Calvin S. to Sarah A. Cadle 9-20-1864
Mullis, Elkana to Nancy Tye 4-8-1853
Murphy, Archibald to Margarett Stephens 1-26-1838
Murphy, Jas. to Elizabeth Perkins 12-22-1877
Murphy, John to Levina Stephens 9-1-1841 (9-2-1841)
Murray, Alfred to Mary Sharp 2-14-1840
Murray, Francis M. to Nancy Perkins 11-15-1870
Murray, George to Mary Ann Haggard 7-28-1854 (7-30-1854)
Murray, George to Winnie Cooper 12-23-1880 (1-1-1881)
Murray, Henderson to Rebecca Delap 11-3-1839
Murray, Jacob to Catharine Brown 12-29-1860 (12-30-1860)
Murray, James C. to Stacy Walden 5-8?-1859
Murray, Jo. H. to Hannah Walden 2-25-1858
Murray, John F. to Marilda Siler 1-3-1850
Murray, John P. to Mary A. Haggard 2-5-1875 (2-7-1875)
Murray, Stephen to Mary J. Tiller 9-25-1857
Murray, Thomas to Mariam Williams 12-27-1839
Murray, William to Sally Hatmaker 3-21-1846
Murray, Wilson to Nancy C. Rollins 2-6-1851
Murray, Wm. F. to Martha J. Young 4-12-1857
Murray, Wm. R. to Nancy Boulton 3-1-1858 (3-11-1858)
Murry, A. to Tabitha Hutson 2-23-1865 (2-24-1865)
Muse, Isaac to Elizabeth Collenls 1-20-1873 (1-22-1873)

Muse, James to Emely Bardling 9-17-1870 (1-22-1871)
Musgrave, Colubus? to Docia Robinson 2-11-1871
Muzingo, Clinton R. to Sarah A. Large 8-9-1865 (no return)
Muzingo, Isaac to Elizabeth Bruce 9-22-1855 (9-23-1855)
Muzingo, Lafayette to Margarett Hill 7-3-1847 (7-4-1847)
Muzingo, Wm. to Mary A. Parker 9-7-1864 (9-8-1864)
Myers, D. T. to Mary Jane Stanford 3-18-1881 (3-20-1881)
Myers, George A. to Mary C. Hunt 8-11-1854
Myers, Milton to Sallie Kincaid 2-16-1876
Myers, Richard to Lavina Whitecotton 6-12-1875 (6-13-1875)
Myers, William to Sousan Butram 7-31-1879
Nance, Alexander to Mary E. Chapman 8-13-1858
Nash, Melkijah V. to Matilda Sharp 7-17-1851 (no return)
Nash, William to Elvina Wells 8-7-1880
Neal, Bartholomew to Kesiah Whitman 7-11-1840 (7-12-1840)
Neal, Isaac to Sarah Gross 10-19-1844 (10-20-1844)
Neal, Jacob W. to Susan Smith 5-30-1861 (6-2-1861)
Nelson, Abraham to Louisa Stout 1-5-1853 (Jan 1853)
Nelson, D. H. to Sallie Ford 10-16-1876 (10-18-1876)
Nelson, Elijah to Barbra Nelson 12-7-1874
Nelson, Enoch to Polley Moore 1-6-1840 (1-9-1840)
Nelson, Henderson to Manerva Brown 3-30-1878 (3-31-1878)
Nelson, P. G. to Barbra Wilson 4-20-1877 (4-25-1877)
Nelson, Peter to Sarelda Wilson 8-16-1880
Nelson, William to Elisabeth Leach 11-19-1876
Nelson, William to Mary Ann Smith 6-12-1841 (6-13-1841)
Nelson, Wm. to Elisabeth Loy 12-24-1864 (12-25-1864)
Newman, John to Sarah Wilhite 5-3-1838 (5-5-1838)
Newport, Asa to Rosanna Greer 11-26-1855 (11-29-1855)
Nicholson, Riley to Emily Sceans 9-9-1849
Nickelson, Speed to Melinda Faulkner 5-30-1844
Nickleson, Fleming to Sarah Skeans 3-28-1844
Nicks, Joseph D. to Emily Shepherd 9-9-1848
Niel, Daniel to Lucinda Flatford 4-24-1855 (4-26-1855)
Niel, Edward to S. Malinda Adkins 9-11-1874 (9-13-1874)
Nix, John to Mary Rains 8-25-1844
Nix, Joseph to Amariah Holt 11-30-1843
Nons, Henry to Polly Smith 12-1838 (no return)
Norman, P. N. to Eliza Wells 9-25-1868
Norton, Peter to Elizabeth Miller 11-6-1856
Nuckells, William to Mary Henderson 10-17-1855
Nunn, Henry to Harrieth Bruce 7-25-1868 (no return)
Oakes, Isaac to Malvinda Ridinour 10-23-1844 (no return)
Oakes, Isaac to Meriah Butler 8-29-1850 (no return)
Oakes, William to Elizabeth Campbell 5-3-1838

Ofallon, P. J. to Lucinda Harris 1-1-1843
Offatt, Nicholas A. to Mary L. Smith 2-25-1869
Oliver, Isom to Nancy Bryant 7-12-1877
Oliver, Luke to Morning Skinner 10-5-1859
Ordens, George W. to Love Claiborn 10-8-1872 (10-13-1872)
Ordens?, Burnett to Susan Orick 2-7-1871
Orice, James to Mary Williams 1-16-1860 (1-18-1860)
Orick, James to Elizabeth Hill 1-14-1875 (1-18-1875)
Orick, John to Cath Lumpkins 2-9-1878 (2-12-1878)
Orick, John to Martha Burchill 5-10-1847 (5-11-1847)
Ousley, George to Ireland Siler 10-28-1838
Ousley, Hesekiah to Hanah Retherford 6-3-1873
Overbay, John to Mary A. Harmon 5-22-1875 (5-23-1875)
Overbey, Herrod to Patty Lynch 2-16-1858 (2-17-1858)
Owen, Thomas to Belinda Polley 11-3-1842
Owens, Jas. to Rebecca Shepard 10-22-1876
Owens, Jourdan to Hannah Fox 8-18-1847 (8-19-1847)
Page, G. F. to Betsy Jane Dossett 2-8-1865 (2-9-1865)
Pangton, John W. to Nancy M. Thomas 6-25-1865 (no return)
Parett, Ewen G. to Margaret Miller 8-17-1860
Parker, Elias to Loraney Wilson 12-181 (12-28-1851)
Parker, Elias to Lorany Wilson 12-22-1851 (no return)
Parker, Elias to Martha McGraw 10-12-1868 (10-18-1868)
Parker, George toOllive Goin 10-3-1865 (10-5-1865)
Parker, James to Elizabeth A. Brooks 2-26-1856 (no return)
Parker, James to Elizabeth Ann Brooks 2-26-1856 (2-28-1856)
Parker, Jas. F. to Nancy Nelson 4-28-1877 (5-2-1877)
Parker, John to Siledia Brooks 7-25-1855 (7-26-1855)
Parker, John to Sledia Brooks 7-25-1855 (no return)
Parker, Robert to Leaner Chapman 4-3-1843 (4-10-1843)
Parker, William to Mary A.a Williamis 8-23-1859 (no return)
Parker, Wm. S. to Sarah Hatmaker 9-24-1869 (9-26-1869)
Parks, J. B. to Mary Snyder 10-10-1869
Parott, Ledford to Martha J. Sharp 7-27-1856
Parrett, Joel to Catherine Marlow 12-9-1838 (1-13-1840)
Parrett, Joel to Catherine Marlow 12-9-1838 (no return)
Parrott, Green to Nettie Hill 2-19-1874
Parrott, R. F. to Lucinda Kesterson 12-22-1876 (12-24-1876)
Parsons, James J. to Mary Harman 2-24-1870 (2-25-1870)
Parton, Shelton to Sally Fraser 10-20-1849 (10-29-1849)
Parton, William to Sarah Day 11-17-1865
Parton, Winston to Elisabeth Powers 11-14-1865
Patterson, Matthew to Isafana McGee 2-29-1856 (3-2-1856)
Patterson, Nicholass to Martha Cross 4-15-1848 (5-18-1848)
Patton, J. O. to Elizabeth J. Smith 5-28-1851 (5-29-1851)

Paul, Doctor to Disa Thompson 4-6-1863 (4-15?-1863)
Paul, Geo. to S. A. Davis 9-2-1875
Paul, George to E. J. Mettinbarger 7-24-1879
Paul, George to Sarah A. Davis 9-2-1875
Paul, James to Malinda Bashim? 5-22-1841 (no return)
Paul, James to Nancy Hale 9-20-1876 (9-21-1876)
Paul, John to Elizabeth Mays 10-20-1868
Paul, John to Louisa Queener 8-18-1858
Paul, Joseph to Sarah Hale 1-1-1873
Paul, Richard to Nancy Parsons 1-14-1869
Peace, Bascum to Louisa Peace 9-10-1876
Peace, Joseph to Rachel Lay 12-23-1869
Peace, Wilson to Mary Powers 11-7-1878
Pearce, Joseph to Narcissa Cole 3-13-1854
Pearce, Peter to Susans Turner 12-4-1870 (1-12-1871)
Pearman, Oglesby to Adaline Harris 6-3-1855
Pebley, Andrew to Rachael Goin 11-27-1840 (11-29-1840)
Pebley, John F. to Mary J. Turner 8-17-1858 (8-18-1858)
Pebley, Wm. to Sarah Woodson 12-8-1869
Pebly, Thomas to Jane Hutson 6-10-1854 (6-11-1854)
Peetree, Isaac to Louisa A. Hudson 6-8-1880
Penberton, David to Elizabeth Martin 8-6-1846 (8-9-1846)
Pennington, Fielding to Elizabeth Chambers 11-9-1839 (11-26-1839)
Pennington, Green to Elisabeth Baird 10-22-1876
Pennington, William to Nancey Jones 9-23-1838
Perkins, Edward to Rebecca Willson 5-9-1854
Perkins, Hiram to Melissa Wilson 6-10-1849
Perkins, J. W. to Tacia Baird 10-1-1880
Perkins, James to Saraha Richmond 1-7-1844
Perkins, Jesse to Louiza Douglass 8-26-1868
Perkins, John L. to Marthy C. Colins 5-27-1862
Perkins, L. D. to Rachel Baird 8-7-1880 (8-8-1880)
Perkins, Lewis to Lurana E. Smith 10-25-1874
Perkins, Peter to Elisabeth Douglass 3-2-1865
Perkins, Peter to Leurana Allen 10-23-1869
Perkins, Peter to Rachel Davis 12-1-1878
Perkins, Peter to Rebecca Wiet 4-2-1846
Perkins, Preston to Sarah E. Martin 12-15-1877
Perkins, Prior to Lucy C. Brooks 9-15-1877
Perkins, Richard M. to Cintha C. Perkins 9-3-1874
Perkins, Riley to Lucy Booth 10-21-1869
Perkins, Solomon to Anna B. Crickmore 1-20-184 (1-23-1849)
Perkins, Squire to Margarett Douglass 4-3-1853
Perkins, Starling M. to Rachel Baird 3-29-1877
Perkins, Sterlin to Emeline Croley 4-10-1879

Perkins, Sterlining to Sarah Smith 10-29-1871
Perkins, Thomas C. to Lyda Chadwell 9-26-1872
Perkins, Thomas to Caytharine Bird 4-2-1845 (4-3-1845)
Perkins, William to Elizabeth Lay 2-4-1846 (2-8-1846)
Perkins, Wm. to Sarah M. Davis 3-20-1856
Perry, O. H. to Susannah Shelton 2-14-1849 (2-20-1849)
Peters, George Smith to Elizabeth Heaton 6-20-1839 (6-21-1839)
Peterson, A. J. to Emily M. Hollingsworth 4-3-1851 (4-5-1851)
Peterson, A. J. to Jane Bowman 9-27-1877
Peterson, John to Ann Ryan 8-5-1847
Peterson, Jos. to Eliza Keeny 7-12-1843
Peterson, Samuel to Martha Dossett 3-29-1869 (4-15-1869)
Peterson, Wilson to Mary Wilhite 9-22-1860 (9-23-1860)
Peterson, Wm. to Sarah Sweatt 12-21-1843 (12-24-1843)
Petree, Adam to Mary Carrol 4-25-1858
Petree, Adam to Senetha Monroe 7-25-1865
Petree, Daniel to Polly Silelr 12-18-1870
Petree, G. W. to Harriet Owens 8-15-1854 (8-20-1854)
Petree, Geo. to Sarah C. Woods 1-10-1876 (1-14-1876)
Petree, George to Mary Ann Green 5-1-1855 (4?-3-1855)
Petree, Isaac to Martha Ford 6-8-1844 (6-13-1844)
Petree, J. C. to Sarah Irvin 9-19-1855 (no return)
Petree, Joel to Minerva Griffet 2-9-1858
Petree, Joel to Ollive Bowlinger 7-23-1864 (7-24-1864)
Petree, John to Catharine Ford 11-16-1850 (11-20-1850)
Petree, John to Caytharine Petree 11-16-1850 (11-21-1850)
Petree, John to Jane Cheek 9-14-1865 (9-21-1865)
Petree, Marian to M. Lawson 10-26-1877
Petree, Sisero to Anna Smith 9-16-1857 (9-17-1857)
Petree, Wm. to Catharine Smith 12-17-1844 (12-26-1844)
Petree, Wm. to Malinda Wells 10-19-1865
Petree, Wm. to Martha J. Williams 12-24-1865
Petrey, Jordan to Mary A. Blakely 4-30-1865
Petrey, Mitchell to R. J. Hudleston 11-17-1880
Petrey, Samuel to Elizabeth Bryant 9-25-1842
Petry, Madison to Sisy Blakely 9-27-1874
Petry, Thomas to Nancy Young 3-22-1846
Petry, Wimer to Elizabeth Silerl 4-21-18877
Philips, Charley to Crasy Dougherty 5-7-1863 (5-10-1863)
Phillips, Benj. to B. Ward 11-26-1875 (11-27-1875)
Phillips, Benjamine to Jane King 12-16-1872 (12-17-1872)
Phillips, Calvin B. to Sarah Johnson 3-25-1866 (4-5-1866)
Phillips, Calvin to Narcis Thompson 10-10-1878 (10-12-1878)
Phillips, Claiborne to Lydia Bullack 6-9-1880 (6-12-1880)
Phillips, Euel to Arminda Sexton 2-11-1860 (2-23-1860)

Phillips, John to Martha McNew 11-13-1863 (no return)
Phillips, Jonathan to Alcey Terry 3-10-1847 (3-20-1847)
Phillips, Joseph to Elizabeth Hicks 7-14-1841 (7-25-1841)
Phillips, Joseph to Josie Adkins 12-13-1875
Phillips, M. L. to Mary C. Hickox 6-6-1843 (6-7-1843)
Phillips, Manuel to Leanner Sexton 2-11-1838
Phillips, Martha Jane to John Stout 6-21-1873
Phillips, Nelson to Rebecca Morgan 5-26-1844
Phillips, P. to E. Dougherty 12-19-1877 (12-25-1877)
Phillips, Rufus to Elizabeth Stout 8-9-1872 (8-15-1872)
Phillips, Thomas to Elizabeth Marlow 3-28-1852
Phillips, Thomas to Ester Terry 3-17-1844
Phillips, Thos. to Susan Dougherty 2-7-1877 (2-8-1877)
Phillips, William to Sarah Lofty 3-8-1870 (3-11-1870)
Pierce, James to P. Nelson 1-8-1856
Pierce, John to America St. John 9-1-1860
Pierce, Peter to Mary Ann Rookard 12-10-1872 (12-11-1872)
Pierce, Peter to Sousan Claiborne 1-12-1880 (1-13-1880)
Pierce, Tho. to Hester Ann Monday 5-21-1859 (5-22-1859)
Pierce, W. A. to Martha McCarty 8-28-1875 (8-29-1875)
Pierce, William to Catharine Richardson 10-5-1846 (10-25-1846)
Pike, Jacob to Jane Benge 8-7-1879
Pilkington, Elbert to Cathrine Cooper 8-16-1865
Pilkington, Joseph A. to Susan Martin 4-20-1843
Ping, Dossony to Ellen Evins 3-16-1854
Pinkleton, John to Elizabeth Jones 2-13-1853
Pitmon, James M. to Polly Glascoke 3-12-1846
Plaster, J. W. to Virginia C. Maupin 12-18-1843 (12-21-1843)
Plaster, Milton to Elizabeth Haytes 8-23-1844 (8-25-1844)
Polly, Pleasant to Mary Lawson 10-10-1850
Polly, Wm. to Mary Lay 7-6-1878
Polston, Green B. to Elizabeth Williams 7-27-1866 (7-29-1866)
Polston, Wm. R. to Elisa J. Blizard 3-4-1875 (3-6-1875)
Polton, Elias to Clara Dougherty 4-8-1878
Porden, Elum to Lucind Hubord 8-26-1845 (no return)
Porter, Harvey to M. E. Johnson 10-20-1875 (10-21?-1875)
Porter, Harvy to M. E. Johnson 10-20-1875 (10-21-1875)
Porter, James H. to Liddy Orice 9-5-1860 (9-3-1860)(sic)
Potter, Andrw to Barbary Pettett 9-2-1871 (9-3-1871)
Poulston, Elias to Gemima Still 12-14-1842 (12-15-1842)
Powel, Forest to Rebecca Teaster 2-21-1852
Powel, James to Martha Jones 4-25-1845
Powell, J. J. to M. J. Wooddard 6-10-1870 (9-1-1870)
Powell, J. P. to Lucy Baker 8-21-1878 (6-18-1879)
Powell, John L. to Nancy Brantly 3-28-1874 (3-29-1874)

Powell, Richd. to Sally Lovett 5-11-1849
Powers, A. K. to Alphare Hatfield 3-29-1865
Powers, Alvin to Martha M. Ready 1-20-1881
Powers, Amos to Elizabeth Blakley 8-1-1868 (8-10-1868)
Powers, Bennett to Eliza S. Chandrin 4-8-1849
Powers, Charles to Nancy Faulkner 7-22-1852
Powers, George to Sallie A. Wilson 5-16-1875
Powers, J. P. to Emaline Roads 12-30-1879
Powers, J. R. to Lucinda Jones 8-1-1879
Powers, Jesse to Susannah Peetry 7-21-1849
Powers, John L. to Louiza Tramell 5-17-1870
Powers, Sampson to Celerria Blakely 9-6-1879
Powers, Speede to Sarah Davis 12-28-1869
Prater, Benjamin to Elizabeth Wright 5-7-1868
Prator, John to Isophine Dossett 11-18-1870 (11-20-1871?)
Presnell, Henry to Manerva Edwards 8-16-1879 (3-17-1879)
Prewet, Warren to Elisabeth J. Osbourne 12-29-1865
Prewett, John to Elizabeth Dooly 12-29-1858
Prewit, Hiram to Chany McKidy 3-12-1846
Prewit, John to Patsy Cox 6-28-1846
Prewit, John to Sarah Ann Nix 2-20-1853
Prewit, Matthias to Jane Cox 4-26-1855
Prewitt, John to Anna Bryant 4-17-1880
Price, Henry to Harriet Hooper 7-4-1864 (7-10-1864)
Price, William to Matilda Adkins 5-10-1840
Prichard, Jack S. to Rebecca Forgeson 12-11-1872
Prichard, Thomas to Louisa Walker 2-27-1842
Prichard, Thos. to July Maze 4-10-1858
Probert, Charles to Olivia Chapman 10-23-1873
Province, J. C. to M. Faulkner 8-10-1879
Province!, William to Jane Smith 11-3-1878
Pruitt, Wimer to Elizabeth Siler 4-21-1877
Queener, Batson to Barbara Clotfelter 7-3-1856
Queener, Caswell to Eveline Walker 3-27-1847
Queener, Daniel to Josephine Queener 8-18-1875 (8-19-1875)
Queener, Danl. to Josephene Queener 8-18-1875 (8-19-1875)
Queener, David to Tabitha M. Queener 7-27-1871 (7-28-1871)
Queener, Franklin to Emma Claibaorn 9-8-1872
Queener, Grandison to Elisabeth E. Perkins 1-10-1864 (1-14-1864)
Queener, Henery to Margaret Jane Clotfelter 1-26-1872 (1-28-1872)
Queener, J. F. to R. E. Rice 8-23-1854 (no return)
Queener, Jacob to Sarah Ann Hope 12-30-1847
Queener, James to Uva Jackson 1-28-1845 (no return)
Queener, Jas. to Emily Hope 4-14-1858 (4-15-1858)
Queener, Jno. E. to Nancy Maupin 1-26-1876 (1-27-1876)

Queener, Johnathan to Elizabeth Bright 7-27-1871
Queener, Jourdan to Theodocia Lindsay 1-18-1855
Queener, Riley to Mary Hope 3-13-1851
Queener, S. D. to Olive Bruce 12-30-1847 (12-31-1847)
Queener, S. R. to M. J. Maupin 6-30-1869 (7-1-1869)
Quener, David to Mary Wilson 7-25-1880
Quener, H. C. to Jane Douglas 2-20-1880 (2-22-1880)
Raine, John to Lanya Martin 10-29-1842
Raine, Samuel to Claris McFarland 5-31-1856
Rainer, Martin to Martha Davis 9-25-1855
Raines, J. B. to Nancy Ray 10-20-1878
Raines, L. T. to Dianah Baird 6-12-1879
Raines, Simeon to Manervy Alder 8-22-1868
Raines, Wilkerson to Darcus Smith 1-22-1870
Raines, Wm. M. to Susan Rains 1-4-1876
Rains, Alison to Lucinda Earley 3-17-1881
Rains, Caswell to Frances Rosier 3-3-1860
Rains, Jackson to Margaret Anderson 6-11-1869
Rains, James C. to Mary Floid 5-23-1858
Rains, James to Sarah Hutson 3-18-1861
Rains, James to Sarah Standly 9-27-1838
Rains, John to Rutha Bunch 3-5-1871
Rains, John to Sarah Miles 4-27-1858
Rains, Robin S. to Mary E. Alder 1-13-1870
Rains, Stephen to Ailsy Johnson 9-2-1858
Rains, Thomas to Mary Clotfelter 2-12-1855 (2-14-1855)
Rains, William to Polly Ann Woods 5-5-1849
Raly, Mathias to Polly Robinson 11-28-1851 (11-30-1851)
Ray, G. W. to Martha J. Vilet 12-22-1863 (12-24-1863)
Reatherford, G. M. to Matilda Rookard 1-9-1870
Reatherford, Rufus to Haney Hibbs 8-28-1874 (8-29-1874)
Reatherford, Thomas J. to Sarah Gayler 3-28-1870
Reatherford, Wm. to Gemima Davis 3-13-1856
Rector, A. J. to Kisiah Ann Fewston 8-8-1870 (8-22-1870)
Rector, Andrew to Frances Rector 11-25-1848 (11-26-1848)
Rector, Joel to Polly Dial 4-26-1845 (5-31-1845)
Rector, Julious to Nancy E. Rector 6-10-1872 (6-16-1872)
Rector, Robert F. to Martha Perkins 2-24-1875 (3-7-1875)
Redenour, Henry to Nancy Cox 4-5-1839 (no return)
Redwine, S. L. to Rissiah Hancock 9-11-1860 (9-16-1860)
Reed, Campbell to Patsey Chitwood 1-23-1840 (1-24-1840)
Reed, E. H. to Mary Smith 5-18-1852 (no return)
Reed, Gorge to Esther Parker 9-11-1849 (no return)
Reed, Isaac to Finby McDonald 6-26-1840 (6-28-1840)
Reed, Joseph B. to Alcy Dabny 8-31-1846 (9-8-1846)

Reedy, J. M. to M. J. Hudson 10-26-1878
Reeves, Columbus to Mary Wilson 10-19-1859
Reeves, George to Sarah Shadowen 1-15-1843
Reeves, John to Catharine Ford 12-28-1854 (no return)
Reeves, Thomas to Ceny Wilson 10-13-1853 (11-1-1853)
Reeves, Wm. to Nancy Longmire 9?-7-1844 (9-15-1844)
Reid, J. Henderson to Mary Lindsay 11-14-1878 (no return)
Reins, Wm. V. to Vicey Smith 10-1-1877
Reives, Frank to Molly Prichard 8-3-1878
Reynolds, Benjamin to Jane Ayers 11-30-1878 (12-1-1878)
Reynolds, Cornelius S. to Elizabeth McCarty 6-2-1838
Reynolds, Elias to E. Chambers 4-18-1880
Reynolds, Elias to Tarey Lay 7-31-1853
Reynolds, Green to Timanda Magusta Woods 3-8-1872 (3-10-1872)
Reynolds, J. B. L. to Nancy Veach 8-2-1880
Reynolds, J. L. to Lucinda Siler 11-23-1880
Reynolds, J. Q. to Hannah Adkins 7-14-1859 (7-15-1859)
Reynolds, John T. to Lucretia Bell Reynolds 6-7-1872 (6-8-1872)
Reynolds, John to Polly Lawson 8-9-1877
Reynolds, Wm. R. to Elizabeth Webb 2-25-1879 (3-2-1879)
Rice, James A. to Marica E. Sexton 10-3-1851
Richardson, Amos to Lucinda Rutherford 8-9-1865
Richardson, Amos to Matilda Wilson 4-3-1851
Richardson, B. F. to A. J. Walton 8-1-1854
Richardson, Benj. to Elizabeth L. Perkins 10-27-1839
Richardson, Daniel C. to Martha Cooper 12-22-1869 (12-26-1869)
Richardson, Daniel to Jane Young 5-10-1845 (5-11-1845)
Richardson, Danl. Jr. to Polley Wilhite 2-10-1838 (2-11-1838)
Richardson, F. to Mary Gray 1-4-1864 (no return)
Richardson, Franklin to Mary Peterson 1-12-1853 (1-13-1853)
Richardson, Henry to Parmelia Hickey 9-1-1845 (no return)
Richardson, Hiram to Martha Pierce 9-6-1843 (no return)
Richardson, Hiram to Nancy Lawson 8-24-1878 (8-25-1878)
Richardson, Hiram to Sarah Williams 12-9-1869 (12-10-1869)
Richardson, J. H. to Nancy Willson 3-6-1858 (3-7-1858)
Richardson, James F. to Martha Gray 6-21-1875 (7-1-1875)
Richardson, John A. to Sue J. Foley 2-3-1876
Richardson, John H. to Manerva Richardson 3-4-1875 (3-6-1875)
Richardson, John H. to Susan Gaylor 6-2-1875 (6-3-1875)
Richardson, L. D. to Milley Shelton 3-20-1842 (no return)
Richardson, Robert to Fannie Smith 10-11-1876
Richardson, S. to Manervy Gray 12-9-1864 (12-11-1864)
Richardson, Thomas B. to Ann Eliza Gray 3-12-1873 (3-16-1873)
Richardson, Wm. H. to Nancy J. Longmire 12-12-1864 (12-20-1864)
Richardson, Wm. W. to Margaret A. Sharp 8-24-1860 (8-26-1860)

Richman, W. D. to M. Douglas 3-31-1878
Richmond, Elias to Catherine Gibson 10-9-1870
Richmond, John R to Polly Davis 2-24-1870
Rickett, Tarlton to Thursay Veach 12-18-1879
Rickett, William to M. J. Bennet 2-18-1875
Ridenhour, John F. to Elizabeth Gray 11-2-1868 (11-5-1868)
Ridenhour, Nathaniel to Elizabeth Jane Pike 2-22-1869
Ridenour, B. F. to Serelda Adkins 2-7-1878 (2-14-1878)
Ridenour, Franka to Tilda Ann Cox 6-19-1879
Ridenour, G. E. to Sarah Brantley 9-17-1842 (no return)
Ridenour, Harvey G. to Lucinda Dagley 7-4-1867
Ridenour, Henry to Celia Miller 3-17-1840
Ridenour, Henry to Nancy J. Dayley 12-23-1856 (12-28-1856)
Ridenour, Henry to Susan Baird 1-8-1876
Ridenour, Jeremiah to Rebecca Day 1-23-1838
Ridenour, L. L. to Laura Ayers 9-6-1879 (10-9-1879)
Ridenour, Mart to Lucy Pyle 10-26-1875
Ridenour, Martin to Lucy Pyle 10-26-1875
Ridenour, Samuel to Seta McFarland 4-7-1854
Ridenour, William to Susan Cox 2-20-1860
Ridenour, Wm. H. to Jane Croley 11-19-1848
Rider, David to Emily Robinson 5-24-1848
Riggs, Edward to Jane Greer 9-4-1847 (9-5-1847)
Riggs, Elias to Jane Leach 12-31-1861 (12-19-1861)
Riggs, James Franklin to Sarah Catherine Morgan 2-5-1881 (2-6-1881)
Riggs, James to Elizabeth Smith 1-2-1844 (1-6-1844)
Riggs, John M. to Mary Cates 8-22-1854 (8-23-1854)
Riggs, John to Mary Hatmaker 7-30-1872 (8-1-1872)
Riggs, Saml. to Hester Ann Chapman 8-26-1869 (8-27-1869)
Riggs, Thomas to Elizabeth Bailey 8-1-1870 (8-3-1870)
Riggs, Thos. to Louisa Dabney 6-11-1857 (6-14-1857)
Riggs, Thos. to Nancy J. Chapman 12-22-1868 (12-23-1868)
Riggs, Vinsen to Mary Ballard 7-20-1844 (7-21-1844)
Riggs, William to Caroline Taylor 8-1-1852 (8-3-1852)
Riggs, William to Catharine Miller 3-18-1854 (3-19-1854)
Right, Huey to M. K. Wilson 6-20-1878
Right, James to C. Wilson 3-17-1853 (no return)
Right, Pharoah to Nancey Blankenship 4-22-1838
Right, Richard to Mary M. Braden 5-9-1863 (5-11-1863)
Roach, Benj. to Ruthey Riggs 3-2-1861
Roach, John to Margaret Anderson 1-26-1847
Roach, John to Marryann Heatherly 6-20-1868 (6-25-1868)
Roach, John to Mary Ann Heatherley 6-20-1868 (6-25-1868)
Roach, John to Sarah M. Nash 2-12-1861 (2-14-1861)
Roach, Manuel to Eliza Thompson 1-5-1848 (1-6-1848)

Roach, Silas L. to Catharine Hutson 9-4-1855 (9-6-1855)
Roach, William to Susan Rebecca Cooper 9-18-1871 (9-19?-1871)
Roach, Wm. to Mary Paul 11-2-1876 (11-3-1876)
Robbins, John to Nancy Harmon 3-3-1849 (3-4-1849)
Robbins, Wm. to Sarah Craig 11-4-1852 (no return)
Robertson, M. C. to Anna Eliza Wheeler 1-22-1850
Robins, Calaway to Lourany Brogans 3-30-1861 (3-31-1861)
Robins, Samiel to Rebecca Foster 11-2-1857 (11-3-1857)
Robins, Samuel to Sarah Lett 11-3-1863
Robins, Wm. to Malinda Fox 2-18-1866
Robison, James A. to Betty Landrum 4-15-1870
Roe, Tho. to Emily Williams 1-21-1858
Roes, Flemon to Jane Campbell 3-2-1865
Roes, Wm. to Matilda Richmond 8-9-1869
Rogers, Benjamin to Elizabeth Adams 11-23-1854
Rogers, D. F. to Sarah Ann Green 1-2-1872 (1-4-1872)
Rogers, D. F. to Sarah J. Dike 8-18-1858 (8-28-1858)
Rogers, David to Cena Williams 2-29-1844
Rogers, George Washington to Catharine Powoel 2-28-1843
Rogers, J. L. to Parlee Willoughby 12-18-1876
Rogers, James A. to Mary E. Cain 2-9-1852 (2-12-1852)
Rogers, James to Rhoda C. Lane 11-16-1868 (11-18-1868)
Rogers, Jas. to S. E. Spangler 3-20-1877
Rogers, Jessee C. to Emly E. Caywood 1-2-1865 (1-6-1865)
Rogers, Patrick H. to Elizabeth Dossett 8-14-1845 (no return)
Rogers, Wm. J. to Elzira Williams 7-14-1838
Rollins, John to A. E. Walker 8-27-1850
Romano, Zachariah to Leah Lay 5-6-1858
Romine, John to Alcy Hunter 11-28-1848 (12-28-1848)
Romines, Allen to Mary Moore 11-2-1849 (11-13-1849)
Rone, G. to S. Whitecotton 6-16-1877 (6-17-1877)
Rookard, Lewis to Eliza J. Branham 7-31-1859
Rose, C. P. to Anna Lawson 11-1-1865
Rose, Jackson to Ann Crowley 12-16-1838
Rose, James to Nancy Lawson 10-21-1857
Rose, Jessee to Elisabeth Hamlin 11-6-1862 (executed?)
Rose, Maticin A. to Malissa Croley 11-1-1865
Rose, Nelson to Elizabeth Polley 2-22-1855
Rose, William to Catherine Jackson 4-14-1848
Rose, Wm. to Nancy Anderson 7-9-1859? (7-9-1856)
Rose, Wm. to Oley Rose 12-7-1856
Rosier, D. C. to Louisa Elkins 4-25-1868
Rosier, Marcus B. to Mary Ann Chapman 12-24-1872 (12-25-1872)
Rosier, Millard to Harriet Jones 7-11-1873 (7-20-1873)
Ross, Henrey to Lucinda Elsnick 5-17-1849

Ross, John S. to Penelope Ann Wheeler 4-17-1852 (4-20-1852)
Ross, John to Nancy Cox 7-30-1584
Ross, Martin L. to Hellen Cary 5-31-1870 (6-7-1870)
Ross, Robert to Martha Dial 12-16-1839 (12-20-1839)
Rosson, Wm. to Hester A. Wright 10-9-1864 (10-13-1864)
Rotten, Eli to Hanna Dawes 4-24-1839 (4-25-1839)
Rouch, G. W. to Charlotty Guan 8-10-1872 (8-1?-1872)
Row, Calvin to Martha Faulkner 11-9-1851
Row, David to America E. Boot 2-16-1860
Rozier, D. H. to Patty Sanders 7-26-1877
Ruckard, James to Elizabeth Boulton 8-9-1852 (8-19-1852)
Runion, Robert to Salena Mays 3-11-1878
Runnold, D. to Nancy Hamlin 2-19-1851
Russel, Thomas to Mary Williams 10-19-1872
Russell, C. D. to Susan E. Izley 1-16-1862
Russell, C. D. to Susan Izley 1-16-1862
Rutherford, Alexander to Minerva Jane Todd 10-15-1851 (no return)
Rutherford, Alfred to Rachel Maloby 4-3-1879
Rutherford, Eliljah to Catharine Campbell 7-29-1875
Rutherford, James to Catharine Rollings 8-20-1851
Rutherford, S. C. to Elisabeth Watson 3-15-1876
Rutherford, Silas to Mary Standle 8-11-1853
Rutherford, Sterling C. to Minty E. Murray 1-2-1859 (1-27-1859)
Rutherford, Wm. to Martha Jordan 4-6-1863 (4-9-1863)
Ryan, Joel to Jane Creekmore 10-19-1843
Ryan, M. V. B. to Carline Elliott 9-10-1865
Ryan, Martin B. to Amelia A. Hatfield 2-22-1849
Ryan, Sant S. to Kitty Ann Hollingsworth 4-1-1854
Ryan, William to Polley Trammell 8-22-1839
Rynolds, C. to Elizabeth Baily 7-16-1854 (no return)
Rynolds, C. to Martha Tidwell 8-10-1854 (8-11-1854)
Salmons, Peter H. P. to Rachel E. McFarland 8-23-1874
Sanders, Abraham to Mary A. Cox 5-12-1859 (1859)
Sanders, Abraham to Susan Wright 6-14-1855 (no return)
Sanders, Eli to Rosanah McFarland 6-29-1857 (7-1-1857)
Sanders, Godfrey D. to Elizabeth Odell 1-9-1866 (1-11-1866)
Sanders, Isaac to Lucinda Geaslin 1-5-1854 (no return)
Sanders, Thos. to H. McFarland 9-7-1877 (9-9-1877)
Sanders, William to Clarissa Glandon 11-11-1841
Saul, Edmond to Tempy Lumpkins 2-22-1872
Savage, A. J. to Sarah Loy 11-3-1851 (11-6-1851)
Sawders, J. G. to Mary Elizabeth Chadwell 10-24-1872
Sawyers, Andrew to Mornin Huddleston 4-21-1864
Sawyers, Samuel to Louisa Woodard 2-13-1853
Scears, Martin to Elizabeth Scears 1-10-1850

Scruggs, William J. to Laura N. Graham 1-25-1881
Scruggs, Wm. J. to Susan M. Qeener? 1-17-1861
Scrutchfield, Jas. to Elizabeth Pierce 11-15-1877
Seabolt, Jacob to Ann Geaseland 9-3-1838 (9-18-1838)
Sears, Thomas to Elzira Adkins 12-7-1870 (12-9-1870)
Seber, Pleasant to Rachel Dougherty 1-15-1880 (1-16-1880)
Secton, Calvin to Nancy Hilton 11-11-1852
Sego?, William to Martha Trammell 9-16-1841
Selvage, Robert to Louisa L. Richardson 10-26-1865
Selvage, Zachariah to Mary Fox 12-23-1856
Sergeant, J. J. to N. W. Jones 1-5-1854 (no return)
Settle, Jno. N. to Dicey M. Smith 11-8-1843 (no return)
Settle, Martin V. to Margaret Shepherd 10-11-1870 (10-16-1870)
Settles, William to Tissie York 12-21-1881 (12-22-1880?)
Sevier, Samuel to Permelia Hibbard 4-24-1838
Sexton, Caswell to Malinda Hix 7-28-1863 (8-13-1863)
Sexton, Daniel to Nancy Emeline Barron 10-3-1872 (10-6-1872)
Shadorie, Joseph to Talitha E. Green 11-22-1864 (12-25-1864)
Shadowins, Andrew to Sarah Norris 8-6-1846
Sharp, Aaron to Nancy Walden 4-7-1853
Sharp, Aron to Emly Adkins (or Stone) 2-18-1871 (2-19-1871)
Sharp, Calvin to Sarah Hatmaker 9-2-1859
Sharp, Cimon to Frankey Sweat 9-17-1873 (9-18-1873)
Sharp, Colson to Anna Snodderly 1-16-1846 (1-18-1846)
Sharp, D. M. to Sarah Smith 1-22-1842 (1-27-1842)
Sharp, Eli to M. J. Hatmaker 11-1-1880 (11-8-1880)
Sharp, F. to Mary Cooper 7-14-1863 (no return)
Sharp, George W. to Louisa J. Longmire 10-23-1850 (10-24-1850)
Sharp, George to Elisabeth Tetters 8-28-1865 (no return)
Sharp, George to Nancy Gayler 2-12-1874
Sharp, Harison to Jane Sharp 10-10-1863 (no return)
Sharp, Henry M. to Eliza Miller 9-17-1856 (9-18-1856)
Sharp, Henry to Catherine Cooper 12-23-1840 (no return)
Sharp, Henry to Sarah Kincaid 11-19-1851 (11-25-1851)
Sharp, Hiram to Melvina Myers 2-7-1881
Sharp, Isham to Nancey Adkins 12-25-1841 (12-30-1841)
Sharp, James F. to Elizabeth Neal 8-9-1854 (8-10-1854)
Sharp, James to Barbara Sharp 9-2-1874 (9-3-1874)
Sharp, James to Mary Allen 11-28-1861 (11-30-1861)
Sharp, James to Neley Sharp 9-14-1858
Sharp, James to Polly Smith 1-8-1846 (1-11-1846)
Sharp, Jno. F. to Mary R. Condady 3-5-1877 (3-15-1877)
Sharp, Joaba to Siothey C. Johnson 4-29-1857 (4-30-1857)
Sharp, John F. to Nancy Wallace 12-28-1872 (12-29-1872)
Sharp, John to Martha Lay 12-31-1878 (1-5-1879)

Sharp, John to Mary Polston 7-17-1876
Sharp, Milton to Minerva Kincaid 4-28-1858 (4-29-1858)
Sharp, Robert B. to Mary C. Rector 8-7-1872 (8-11-1872)
Sharp, Silas to Anne? Hutsell 12-19-1868 (12-23-1868)
Sharp, Thomas to Margaret Karr 2-22-1847
Sharp, Tilmond to Cerena Adkins 12-26-1846 (12-27-1846)
Sharp, William D. to Manervy Sparks 9-12-1874 (9-17-1874)
Sharp, William H. to Sarah J. Kincaid 9-22-1851 (9-25-1851)
Sharp, William to Martha Wilson 5-29-1875
Sharp, Wm. D. to Julia Miller 5-21-1845 (5-27-1845)
Sharp, Wm. F. to Minerva J. Myers 11-5-1861 (11-14-1861)
Sharp, Wm. M. to Saraha Cravens 2-5-1877 (2-8-1877)
Sharp, Wm. R. to Eliza Jane Lay 10-6-1879 (10-1?-1879)
Sharp, Wm. R. to Malinda Bullock 9-11-1880 (9-23-1880)
Sharp, Win. to Elizabeth J. Alenl 11-28-1861 (11-29-1861)
Sharp, Win. to Permela Walden 2-15-1863 (executed?)
Shaufner, Berry to Sarah Shelby 11-16-1852 (11-17-1852)
Shelby, Frances to Lemuel Hill 3-20-1856
Shelby, J. M. to Elizabeth Jones 5-5-1878
Shelby, Samuel to Sally McCully 1-4-1843 (no return)
Shelly, Nathan to Nancy Faulkner 12-23-1843 (12-24-1843)
Shelton, Eli to J. E. Smith 2-3-1854 (no return)
Shelton, Hillard to Mary Nelson 1-2-1855 (no return)
Shelton, James M. to M. J. Rice 8-8-1855
Shepherd, Benjamin to Nancy Milton 3-19-1853
Shepherd, J. R. to Calls Chapman 7-11-1878 (7-13-1878)
Shepherd, Thomas to Sarah Lunsford 10-13-1873 (11-10-1873)
Shlopen, Phillip to Sarah McGraw 2-20-1864 (2-21-1864)
Shoopman, R. to Margarett Harness 6-13-1839
Short, John H. to Rhoda Smith 2-18-1865 (3-2-1865)
Shown, A. W. to Nancy Heatherley 7-1-1871 (7-2-1871)
Shown, William C. to J. C. Gross 1-1-1875 (1-3-1875)
Shown, Wm. C. to Mahulda Lindsay 11-16-1849 (11-18-1849)
Shumake, William to Cornelia E. Reed 7-20-1842 (no return)
Shumate, Carr to Sarah Maupin 9-5-1839 (9-12-1839)
Shumate, Sampson to Polley Barber 8-11-1840 (8-15-1840)
Silcox, Granvill to Lyda Marcum 3-4-1878
Siler, Adam to Mary Jane Siler 10-26-1873
Siler, Adam to Nancy Snider 9-14-1856
Siler, Alvis to Rachel Campbell 3-16-1851
Siler, Elislha to Elizabeth Faulkner 8-8-1850
Siler, F. M. to Mary Brumet 9-5-1860 (Sept)
Siler, Green to Rachal Murray 5-15-1873
Suter, Hase to Mary Seirs 7-13-1873
Siler, Jacob to Margaret Petree 1-5-1848

Siler, James B. to Nancy Siler 2-14-1869
Siler, James S. to Roana Elison 4-25-1870
Siler, Jno. to Harriett Owens 3-31-1844
Siler, John M. to Polly Ann Stanfill 9-29-1846
Siler, Joseph to Christena Adkins 3-31-1849 (4-1-1849)
Siler, L. D. to S. J. Hamby 8-23-1879
Siler, L. F. to Nancy Reeder 10-28-1877
Siler, L. L. to C. J. Bird 10-21-1874
Siler, Ledford to Sary Blakely 1-4-1880
Suter, Perry to Margaret Bolton 12-9-1870
Siler, Sterling to Josepine Suter 11-24-1880
Siler, T. E. B. to Nannie Stanfill 8-15-1878
Suter, Thomas to Rachel Ellison 8-14-1879
Siler, William to Elizabeth Snyder 11-15-1855
Siler, William to Nancy Lawson 11-16-1854
Siler, Wm. to Susan S. Bennett 3-14-1880
Siles, Benjamin to Martha Holt 12-27-1848
Siles, Benjamin to Martha Holt 9-7-1848 (no return)
Silor, Milford to Nancy Lawson 2-27-1879
Simpkin, William to Manerva Dossett 7-18-1841 (no return)
Skeen, James R. to Armild Owens 1-29-1854
Skeens, Francis M. to Agey Rogers 4-7-1864
Skeens, John to Juli Ann Cader 7-20-1871
Slaven, Elitia to Polly Sweet 3-8-1847
Smiddy, Benj. to Adaline Petit 3-16-1878
Smiddy, Calvin to Elizabeth Hicks 3-19-1844 (3-28-1844)
Smiddy, Calvin to Elizabeth Petit 4-11-1861
Smiddy, Calvin to Julia David 3-15-1878
Smiddy, Isaac to Elizabeth McFarland 7-24-1839 (7-28-1839)
Smiddy, James to Elizabeth Cooper 12-25-1850 (12-26-1850)
Smiddy, James to Hanner Webb 12-20-1865
Smiddy, John to Ailsy Woods 12-24-1870 (12-27-1870)
Smiddy, John to Anna Kesterson 4-22-1875
Smiddy, Reubin to Marth Witt 2-12-1878
Smiddy, Rewbin to B. A. Phillips 2-27-1844 (3-9-1844)
Smiddy, Ruben to Easter Hicks 7-19-1856 (7-29-1856)
Smidy, James F. to Polly Woods 5-3-1870 (5-5-1870)
Smith, A. D. to Summerfield Miller 11-6-1841 (11-10-1841)
Smith, A. J. to Margaret Maupin 6-30-1854 (July 1854)
Smith, A. J. to Vicey Black 5-3-1854 (5-14-1854)
Smith, Abraham to Frankey Jan Brook 2-17-1870
Smith, Alvis to M. A. Henager 11-1-1880 (11-22-1880)
Smith, Anderson to Melinda Dossett 8-18-1840 (no return)
Smith, Andrew to Sarah Meadors 4-5-1852 (4-8-1852)
Smith, Anthoney to Mary Jane Leach 9-29-1869

Smith, Archd. to Mary M. Maupin 3-21-1853 (3-22-1853)
Smith, Benjamin to Elizabeth Boid 5-10-1869
Smith, Benjamin to Nancy Miller 4-26-1864 (5-2-1864)
Smith, Brick M. to Frances Lassly 7-27-1872 (8-2-1872)
Smith, Calvin to Rebeca Penington 7-31-1856 (8-31-1856)
Smith, Caswell to Sarah Ann Read 7-27-1850 (no return)
Smith, Crank to Emely Sweatt 9-5-1872
Smith, David to Catharine St. John 8-30-1845 (no return)
Smith, E. to Polly Chapman 8-8-1845 (9-10-1845)
Smith, Edward to Jane Smith 5-5-1839 (5-8-1839)
Smith, Euracus to Harriet Bratcher 6-15-1877 (6-17-1877)
Smith, Ewel to Julyan Owens 8-10-1848 (no return)
Smith, Ewel to Zephry Lawson 11-10-1864
Smith, F. A. to Jane Morrow 8-1-1868 (8-2-1868)
Smith, Frederick to Pricilla Hutson 2-19-1846
Smith, Fredrick to Mary Sharp 3-22-1881 (4-3-1881)
Smith, G. W. to Julia Ann Smith 2-10-1845 (2-13-1845)
Smith, George to Kisiah Neal 8-4-1849 (8-5-1849)
Smith, George to Rebecca Richardson 3-2-1861 (3-23-1861)
Smith, Granville to Elizabeth Cates 3-7-1857 (3-8-1857)
Smith, Hanson to Hannah Gibson 4-7-1840 (4-9-1840)
Smith, Horace to Sophia Kincade 2-3-1858 (2-4-1858)
Smith, Hunly to Susan Miller 2-9-1841 (2-11-1841)
Smith, Isaac S. to Synthia Broyles 2-6-1881
Smith, J. L. to Mary Vinsant 11-9-1875
Smith, J. B. to Martha Leach 5-16-1879
Smith, J. N. to Lucinda Lay 11-25-1880
Smith, James E. to Catharine McNew 11-15-1859 (11-19-1859)
Smith, James M. to Winna Lay 2-26-1857
Smith, James to Nancy Debley 6-7-1846 (no return)
Smith, Jeremiah to Eliza Jane Lay 3-27-1873
Smith, Jesse to Ann Thompson 4-10-1839 (4-11-1839)
Smith, Joel to Flora T. Smith 6-10-1879 (6-11-1879)
Smith, John E. to Elvina Butler 9-1-1853 (9-2-1853)
Smith, John T. to Sarah Irwine 8-19-1878 (9-5-1878)
Smith, John to Ann Skiliner 8-17-1848
Smith, John to Cinthia Spangler 3-8-1880 (3-14-1880)
Smith, John to Martha St. John 10-14-1848 (10-15-1848)
Smith, John to Mary A. Honeycutt 12-27-1878 (12-29-1878)
Smith, John to Nancey W. Cotten 11-14-1840 (11-15-1840)
Smith, John to Olley Jones 4-17-1842
Smith, John to Sarah Orrick 12-24-1879 (12-26-1879)
Smith, Joseph M. to Nancy Hackter 11-14-1865 (no return)
Smith, Joseph M. to Sarah Peterson 9-8-1852 (9-11-1852)
Smith, Joseph to Nancey Baker 6-8-1840 (6-15-1840)

Smith, Josiah to Elizabeth Nettles 2-28-1850
Smith, Josiah to Hester A. Siler 5-5-1878
Smith, Josiah to Phoeba Croley 11-29-1865
Smith, Lee J. to Margaret Boyd 8-22-1860 (8-23-1860)
Smith, Levi to Martha Reed 12-28-1850 (1-2-1851)
Smith, Marcelous M. to Jane S. Woodson 10-31-1868 (11-4-1868)
Smith, Milton to Adaline Norton 8-6-1857
Smith, N. B. to Lousinda White 2-13-1871
Smith, O. T. to Eliza Jane Queener 3-4-1872 (3-14-1872)
Smith, Pascal to Susan McClary 10-14-1841 (no return)
Smith, Pleasent to Sarah H. Heninger 5-6-1872 (5-12-1872)
Smith, Richard to M. J. Boyd 8-23-1877 (8-25-1877)
Smith, Richard to Rachael Terry 1-8-1839 (1-16-1839)
Smith, Ridser? to Milly Ann McCoy 8-15-1848 (8-20-1848)
Smith, Robt. H. to Martha J. Chapman 3-13-1849
Smith, Rufus K. to Maria Maupin 2-1-1852 (2-10-1852)
Smith, Samuel to Susan J. Campbell 7-18-1852
Smith, Sterlin to Polly McNeely 7-19-1850 (7-20-1850)
Smith, Sterling to Margarett Queener 10-24-1851 (10-25-1851)
Smith, Stout to M. E. Kelso 3-25-1869 (3-26-1869)
Smith, Tho. A. to Susan Hill 1-26-1857 1857
Smith, Thomas M. to Delpha Hackler 1-14-1863
Smith, Thomas to Martha W. Cooper 7-24-1851 (7-31-1851)
Smith, Thos. A. to Hannah Riggs 9-2-1875 (9-3-1875)
Smith, Thos. W. to Hester Kincaid 2-15-1862 (no return)
Smith, Uriah to S. Douglas 6-21-1877
Smith, W. M. to N. J. Hutson 4-28-1868 (4-30-1868)
Smith, William A. to Susan McFarland 8-10-1871
Smith, William H. to E. S. Kincaid 10-24-1849
Smith, William to Elizabeth Cliborn 7-24-1851 (7-28-1851)
Smith, William to Jane Harmon 5-16-1880 (5-23-1880)
Smith, Wm. Ad. to Phebe Housley 11-6-1879
Smith, Wm. Mabory to Amanda McGlothlin 1-9-1872 (1-29-1872)
Smith, Wm. W. to M. V. Richardson 8-1-1876 (8-3?-1876)
Smith, Wm. to Lockey Cox 9-5-1843 (9-10-1843)
Smith, Wyatt to Lucretia Smith 10-24-1854 (10-26-1854)
Smithy, Lewis to Sarah Ayers 9-7-1878 (9-8-1878)
Smitty, Calvin to Lucy Reynolds 4-8-1880
Snodderly, George to Parlena Wilson 11-6-1864 (11-7-1854)
Snodderly, H. to Nancy Lett 4-23-1855 (5-3-1855)
Snodderly, John to Eliza Sharp 2-14-1846 (2-8?-1846)
Snodderly, Rice to Lucy Irvin 3-5-1855
Snyder, H. F. to Susan J. Perkins 8-27-1864 (8-28-1864)
Snyder, J. R. to Malinda C. Ivey 3-3-1872
Solomon, Wm. to Mary Angoner 5-6-1850

Sosbe, Joshua M. to Eleneory Ragan 1-29-1879
Spangler, John to Eaeley Childres 8-1-1859 (no return)
Spangler, Sylvester to Catharine Dunn 12-21-1870 (12-23-1870)
Spangler, Sylvester to Ellen Bratcher 4-10-1880 (4-11-1880)
Sparks, Rufus to Cally Davis 9-20-1878 (10-3-1878)
Spitta, Green B. to Hannah Miller 3-8-1842 (3-10-1842)
Sprinkle, Jacob to Iduma Bowling 1-12-1878
St. John, Avis to Vire Fur 8-17-1859 (8-21-1859)
St. John, John to Sarah M. Meritt 9-10-1878 (9-12-1878)
St. John, Wm. to Lucinda Norton 4-30-1854
St. John, Wm. to Martha Grant 8-1-1863
St. John, Wm. to Mary Corder 6-1-1861 (6-15-1861)
Stair, Wm. F. to Martha Baxter 12-24-1872 (12-25-1872)
Stamper, Jesse B. to Martha Smimth 6-21-1840
Standfill, James R. to Sefroney Adkins 1-22-1846
Standley, Reuben to Nancey Branham 2-20-1840
Standly, R. S. to Rosey Hix 8-3-1846
Stanfield, Letcher to Hannah Beard 1-9-1843 (1-19-1843)
Stanfill, H. H. to Rachael Low 5-28-1857
Stanfill, Hiram to Lucy Perkins 4-28-1849 (5-3-1849)
Stanfill, Isham J. to Orlena Lawson 10-2-1860 (10-4-1860)
Stanfill, James to Lucinda Broyles 1-29-1846
Stanfill, James to Nancy Lay 4-26-1872
Stanfill, John to Lucy Vatch 12-7-1850
Stanfill, Lewis to Cintha Lay 5-6-1868 (5-7-1868)
Stanfill, Lewis to E. S. Lay 6-15-1877
Stanfill, Melton to Rebecca J. Collins 1-20-1865
Stanfill, Milton to Rachael Beard 1-13-1842 (2-3-1842)
Stanfill, Sampson to Celia Carroll 12-18-1869 (12-19-1869)
Stanfill, William M. to Catherine Broyles 9-19-1874
Stanford, W. C. to M. A. Herron 2-14-1880 (2-15-1880)
Stanley, D. M. to Nancey Archer 14-1842 (no return)
Stanley, Rueben to Nancy Branham 2-20-1840
Stansbury, Solomon to Jane Beams 4-5-1839
Stapleton, James to Jane Parton 9-1-1848
Steel, J. P. M. to Louisa Miller 1-28-1880
Steele, Randolph M. to Minerva J. Howel 3-13-1854
Steers, William to Mary Lamare 4-26-1869 (4-27-1869)
Stephens, James to Hannah Thomas 10-9-1843 (10-10-1843)
Stephens, Joel to Jane Thomas 5-30-1839
Stephens, Welcome to Margarett Williamson 8-23-1839 (9-5-1839)
Stepp, John to Hannah Barbey 2-14-1870
Stewart, Andrew to Nancy Arther 12-6-1847
Stewart, Robert to Susan Faulkner 2-10-1839
Stiner, Eli to Luisa Jane Heathery 6-10-1841 (6-22-1841?)

Stokes, H. S. to Mary C. Turnbill 5-1-1879
Stokes, W. S. to A. B. Bonham 5-28-1879 (5-29-1879)
Stokes, Wyatt to Nancy Jane Harmon 10-20-1847
Stone, David to Emly J. Adkins 4-10-1864 (no return)
Stone, Henry P. to Lassia E. Smith 7-1-1869
Stooksberry, Robert to Jane Sharp 7-27-1846 (8-5-1846)
Stooksbury, Samuel to Sally Sharp 12-12-1846 (12-15-1846)
Stouksbury, Alvis to E. J. Irwine 7-23-1878 (7-28-1878)
Stout, G. D. to Margaret Milton 9-10-1846 (no return)
Stout, James M. to Elizabeth Fox 1-7-1856
Stout, Jno. H. to Orlena Wilhite 10-18-1844 (no return)
Stout, John to Martha Jane Phillips 6-21-1873 (6-26-1873)
Stout, Matison to Orpha Allbright 3-15-1849
Stout, Scott to Eliza Carroll 2-17-1877 (2-18-1877)
Stout, Thomas to Marya Irwine 5-27-1872 (8-19-1872)
Stout, W. F. to M. L. Ayers 4-21-1873 (April 1873)
Stout, William to Mary Love Petree 12-21-1874 (12-24-1874)
Stover, James to Sarah Brown 8-2-1854 (8-3-1854)
Strader, Daniel to Anna Davis 12-10-1873 (12-14-1873)
Strader, Jesse to Lucy Ann McClain 12-19-1872
Strader, John to Sarah Rutherford 11-15-1872 (11-17-1872)
Stratton, John O. to Susan Wilson 1-3-1880
Stringer, James M. to Manday McFall 8-30-1842
Strong, William to Elizabeth Smiddy 1-6-1871
Strunk, Abram to Melinda Waters 10-31-1849
Strunk, Daniel to Melinda Ryan 3-24-1849 (3-27-1849)
Strunk, James to Polley King 5-12-1842
Strunk, Noah to E. J. Heart 3-3-1878
Strunk, William M. to Melinda Ligo 10-15-1840
Stukesberry, R. C. to Orlena Irwiwn 11-31-1863 (no return)
Sulbain, James F. to Jane M. Skeans 4-3-1842
Sulcatt?, William V. to Mariaha Myers 7-6-1870 (7-7-1870)
Sullivan, Isaac to Susasn Macmand 9-29-1850
Summers, L. D. to Catharine Malicote 7-20-1859
Sumner, R. to Ardelo Rector 8-20-1870 (8-29-1870)
Sumner, Samuel to Christina Brown 1-24-1846
Sumter, Francis M. to Rebecca Arton 11-27-1848
Surritt, Jno. to Mary E. Madors 11-30-1843 (no return)
Suttle?, John to Cilly Ann Bratcher 4-4-1838 (4-5-1838)
Sutton, Henry H. to Heton L. Kincaid 6-10-1865 (6-13-1865)
Sutton, J. W. to Mary E. Faulkener 1-15-1869
Sutton, Liberty L. to Jane McFarland 9-30-1839
Sutton, Samuel to Frances C. Griffit 9-7-1868
Sutton, Shadrach to Polly Henderson 10-19-1848 (10-20-1848)
Sutton, Sterling to Sarah Ann Cox 9-21-1878 (9-22-1878)

Swain, Jesse to Polly Ball 1-9-1849 (1-11-1849)
Sweat, Calvin to Melvina Todd 10-10-1845 (no return)
Sweat, Dabney to Elisabeth Sweat 8-17-1878 (8-22-1878)
Sweat, Frank to Anna Davis 10-21-1871 (10-22-1871)
Sweat, Frank to Mary Jane Draper 8-27-1873
Sweat, Franklin to Rachel Baily 7-12-1879 (7-13-1879)
Sweat, Granville to Louisy Dimerson? 12-28-1880
Sweat, Henderson to Rebecca Slaven 10-15-1848
Sweat, Jno. Q. A. to Mary McCarty 11-7-1845 (no return)
Sweat, Robert to Sarah Alder 2-10-1870 (2-11-1870)
Sweat, Wm. to Evey Jane Spangler 11-29-1870 (12-6-1870)
Sweat, Wm. to Frances McCarty 7-29-1843 (7-30-1843)
Sweaten, Robert to Jane Thompson 12-30-1865 (12-31-1865)
Sweaton, Edward to Jane Pinkleton 1-15-1840
Sweatt, John to Jane Abbett 9-10-1848
Sweatt, John to Sarah Wells 5-11-1872 (5-14-1872)
Syler, H. T. to Elender A. Davis 8-21-1857
Tabor, David to Clarisa Phillips 9-17-1859 (9-18-1859)
Tacket, David to Nancy V. Meriday 12-26-1860 (12-27-1860)
Tacket, James B. to Biddy Hatfield 11-26-1844 (11-27-1844)
Tankestley, William to Anna Beams? 4-14-1842
Tay, Samuel to Louiza Lawson 9-15-1868 (9-17-1868)
Tayler, Richmond to Sarah Ryan 12-17-1841
Taylor, Campbell to Mary Henderson 8-6-1841
Taylor, Danl. to Nancey J. Angel 8-1-1877 (8-2-1877)
Taylor, David B. to Emily Faubus 8-9-1865
Taylor, Ewin to Caroline Rooark 9-11-1854
Taylor, G. M. to Roda Richardson 11-5-1859 (11-6-1859)
Taylor, George M. to Jane Rozier 11-18-1865 (11-19-1865)
Taylor, H. C. to F. V. Tye 1-11-1870
Taylor, John B. to Sarah C. Dotson 12-13-1880
Taylor, John to Elizabeth Cravin 7-25-1859 (7-26-1859)
Taylor, Jonathan to Elizabeth Richardson 6-18-1856 (6-19-1856)
Taylor, William M. to Elizabeth Graham 3-13-1869 (3-14-1869)
Taylor, William W. to Vicy Ausmus 9-27-1865
Taylor, Wm. to Mary Miller 12-29-1864
Taylor, Wm. to Nancy Dotson 1-24-1878
Teague, G. C. to Martha Cambdin 8-20-1865
Teague, James to Margaret Lamdin 8-15-1869
Teaster, Hiram to Angeline Dowel 12-24-1857 (no return)
Teaster, Nathaniel to Louisa Hill 9-26-1857 (9-27-1857)
Terrell, John to Jane Floid 3-10-1857
Terrey, Martin to Nancey Thompson 9-17-1842 (no return)
Terry, Martin to Nancy Thompson 9-17-1843 (no return)
Thomas, A. D. to Sally Wilson 3-1-1869 (3-2-1869)

Thomas, Aaron to Mary Broyles 8-30-1855
Thomas, Adnejoh? to Mary Riggs 7-27-1877 (7-29-1877)
Thomas, Adonijah to Mary Ann Lovely 8-5-1847
Thomas, Danl. to Nancy Broyles 1-2-1852 (1-22-1852)
Thomas, F. M. to M. Ridenour 9-6-1877
Thomas, G. W. to Mina Flatford 9-7-1852 (no return)
Thomas, Hiram to Melinda Bodkin 11-28-1839
Thomas, Isaac J. to Jane Dossett 2-1-1851 (no return)
Thomas, Isaac to Winney West 3-28-1847
Thomas, J. P. to Hazy Weever 10-4-1870 (10-5-1870)
Thomas, J. S. to Sarah J. King 12-30-1880
Thomas, James B. to Elisabeth Robinson 1-7-1864 (1-10-1864)
Thomas, James to Susan Craig 4-7-1856 (no return)
Thomas, John to Barbary Grimes 12-16-1839 (12-19-1839)
Thomas, John to Pollyann Price 7-16-1865 (7-10?-1865)
Thomas, John to Sarah Smith 8-29-1868 (9-7-1868)
Thomas, Mary to Richard Williamson 12-1-1880
Thomas, Michael to N. J. Ridenour 11-2-1879
Thomas, S. W. to Lavina Boatright 7-2-1855
Thomas, S. W. to Matilda Row 5-27-1873
Thomas, Sherd to Elizabeth Ridenour 9-6-1877
Thomas, Stephen to Sarah Reed 7-3-1843 (7-5-1843)
Thomas, Wyly to Scinthia Polly 12-3-1843 (12-7-1843)
Thomerson, A. to Jane Sweaton 2-20-1855 (8-8-1855)
Thompson, Berry to Celia Lay 9-20-1844 (10-2-1844)
Thompson, H. to Polly Hatfield 5-19-1853 (7-11-1853)
Thompson, James to C. M. Rowlet 10-19-1855
Thompson, James to Kisiah Potter 1-22-1846
Thompson, Jery to Nancy Baird 3-27-1878 (3-28-1878)
Thompson, Levi to Elisabeth Pane 4-15-1863
Thompson, Thomas to Polly Ann 12-9-1852 (no return)
Thompson, Wm. to Rachael Tacaked 8-4-1858 (8-5-1858)
Thompson, Wm. to Uria Mowell 3-7-1879
Thornton, William to Sarah Ann Davis 6-16-1839
Thurmond, J. W. W. to Maggie E. Stathem 12-26-1870 12-29-1870)
Tibbs, Robert to Anna E. Douglass 12-13-1875 (12-14-1875)
Tidwell, Geo. to Sarah Boshears 12-15-1877
Tidwell, William to Martha Reynolds 10-17-1872
Tiller, F. M. to Kisiah Gross 6-1851
Tiller, G. W. to Sousan Vinsant 12-19-1878 (12-22-1878)
Tiller, H. C. to Elisabeth Richardson 7-29-1863 (8-9-1863)
Tiller, Henry C. to Emily Hutson 7-31-1849 (8-14-1849)
Tiller, J. B. to Elisa Robbins 10-13-1877 (3-9-1878)
Tiller, Joseph L. to M. J . Heatherly 1-6-1880 (Jan 1880)
Tiller, N. to J. Wilson 4-20-1877 (4-21-1877)

Tiller, W. P.? to Jane Adkins 4-12-1856 (4-13-1856)
Tiller, William F. to Lucretia Longmire 4-14-1874 (4-19-1874)
Tiller, Williey to Lucinda Harrison 2-5-1853 (2-6-1853)
Tople, George P. to Martha J. Smith 12-8-1873
Trail, Jamese to Susan Prock 1-18-1850
Trammel, James to Rebecca Hamby 6-10-1846 (no return)
Trammel, Jarrett to Lavenia Marcum 5-18-1839 (5-19-1839)
Trammel, M. W. to Louisa J. Perkins 12-15-1856 (no return)
Troutman, J. C. to Ephy Siler 9-13-1877
Tucker, J. M. to Martha Gray 10-9-1839
Tudor, George to Sarah Blevins 8-1-1846 (no return)
Tullock, Z. T. to Tabitha Rogers 3-3-1870
Turner, Elihu to Dicy Richardson 3-4-1850 (3-10-1850)
Turner, Elihue to Dicy Richardson 3-8-1848 (3-10-1848)
Turner, James A. to Elisabeth J. Dossett 2-28-1865 (3-2-1865)
Turner, James to Sally Williamson 9-7-1846 (10-4-1846)
Turner, John to Mary Pearce 5-6-1844 (5-19-1844)
Turner, P. B. to Mary Sweat 12-7-1849 (12-9-1849)
Turner, Reuben to Alcy McGlauthlin 2-4-1856 (2-6-1856)
Turner, Valentine to Lucinda Malone 11-20-1843 (no return)
Turner, William to Ceila Shepherd 7-21-1880 (7-22-1880)
Turner, William to Edy J. Butler 7-5-1855 (no return)
Turpin, Samuel B. to Manda Gooden 11-4-1848
Tussy, Jacob L. to Leatha Forbes 5-15-1865
Tuttle, J. M. to Mary J. S. Bow[ling 3-2-1874
Tuttle, Peter to Elizabeth Smithi 4-8-1841
Tye, Henry H. to Lucy B. Ward 12-30-1859
Tye, Hiram to Nancy Siler 9-28-1879
Tyre, James R. to Orelena Baker 2-27-1865
Umphres, Charles to Leuiza Raines 2-20-1870 (2-22-1870)
Underwood, J. W. to Nancy McFarlalnd 9-19-1854
Usher, Geo. to L. A. Baily 2-12-1875
Valentine, Henry to Frances Lovett 1-7-1847
Vanderpool, John to Anna Dossett 6-19-1844 (6-24-1844)
Vanderpool, John to Polly Baily 1-15-1847
Vanderpool, Samuel to Nancy Brown 12-7-1848 (12-8-1848)
Vania, Wadrick H. to Martha J. Cears 6-11-1852
Vanover, Andrew to Nancy Kith? 6-8-1859
Vaughn, J. C. to Jennie Foley 3-7-1879
Vernon, James A. to Mary E. Siler 7-26-1874
Vess, Robert to Charity Powers 12-26-1877
Vindsant, Richard to Martha J. Perkins 3-23-1859 (3-24-1859)
Vinsaint, J. M. to L. V. Tiller 2-4-1874 (2-15-1874)
Vinsaint, L. P. to E. Smith 4-23-1874 (4-24-1874)
Vinsant, J. L. to Nancy A. Walker 7-3-1869 (7-6-1869)

Vinsant, James M. to Liddy V. Turner 2-14-1874 (2-15-1874)
Vinsant, James to Elizabeth Douglass 10-2-1844 (10-3-1844)
Vinsant, L. P. to Elizabeth Smith 4-23-1874 (4-24?-1874)
Vinsant, Washington to Lavina Richardson 5-17-1845 (5-18-1845)
Vinzant, Daniel to Susan Page 9-20-1838 (9-21-1838)
Vinzant, G. W. to Mary Richardson 5-17-1854 (5-18-1854)
Vinzant, Henry L. to Malvina Ponder 10-15-1846 (10-25-1846)
Vinzant, Lemuel P. to Mary Walker 3-5-1851 (3-6-1851)
Violet, John to Nancy Cox 11-26-1877
Violett, Wm. to Harriet Burress 4-9-1873
Vowel, James to Jane Mozier 9-26-1863
Vowel!, James to E. J. Bridgman 7-8-1855
Wadkins, Henry to Rachael Tidwell 5-31-1861 (6-6-1861)
Wadkins, James to Elender Hutson 1-1-1865
Wadson, John to Easter Rutherford 9-2-1864
Waisman, J. A. to E. Hollingsworth 6-10-1851
Waisman, James A. to Bell E. Wheeler 8-16-1864
Walden, A. C. to Mary Bell Ledford 4-1-1879 (4-3-1879)
Walden, Benjamin to Elizabeth Gaylor 4-8-1855
Walden, Evin to Nancy Sharp 4-28-1853
Walden, Felix to America Hatfield 8-23-1870
Walden, Georg to Hanah Gaylor 1-24-1861
Walden, James Jr. to Jane Rose 9-2-1852
Walden, John H. to Jane York 1-29-1871
Walden, Mellvill to Deily Rose 2-6-1851
Walden, William to Elizabeth Guffe 11-3-1848
Walden, Wm. to Arrena Phillips 5-26-1865
Watdon, Ben F. to Martha Balton 5-28-1865
Walker, A. A. to Joanah England 1-16-1875
Walker, Absolum to Susan O. Haggard 12-25-1847 (no return)
Walker, J. H. to Josephine E. Bibb 5-4-1868
Walker, James to Cintha Reeves 7-1857 (7-24-1857)
Walker, Lafayett to Mary Ann Hatmaker 5-17-1869 (5-20-1869)
Walker, R. to Jane Miller 1-24-1861
Walker, T. H. to Susan Wilhite 3-20-1869
Walker, William to Anna Hampton 7-19-1848 (7-20-1848)
Walker, Willson to Minerva Smith 3-5-1865
Walker, Wm. H. to M. Kincaid 10-12-1854 (10-19-1854)
Wallace, Johnson to Milley Murry 11-5-1864 (11-6-1864)
Wallace, Joseph to Maranda German 12-17-1862 (12-19-1862)
Wallace, Robert to Peggy Brown 7-21-1860
Walton, G. W. to Catharine Smith 4-4-1852 (4-5-1852)
Walton, General to Elizabeth Smith 2-5-1881
Walton, J. P. to E. J. Tackett 4-12-1875 (4-13-1875)
Walton, Samuel to Nancy Huckaby 1-11-1856 (1-27-1856)

Walton, William to Tennessee Sexton 3-17-1876 (3-19-1876)
Ward, Andrew to M. E. Webb 2-22-1881 (2-23-1881)
Ward, F. to B. A. Phillips 8-23-1878 (8-26-1878)
Ward, Jahel to Nancy Jane Ward 4-8-1872 (4-9-1872)
Ward, John A. to Clara Phillips 3-5-1856 (no return)
Ward, Martin to Polly Ann McKamy 6-7-1854 (6-29-1854)
Ward, Michael to Sousan Tackett 10-24-1878
Ward, Michal to Manervey McGee 8-8-1868 (8-16-1868)
Ward, Wm. to Eliza J. Kesterson 8-1-1855 (8-9-1855)
Ward, Wm. to Mima Kenady 12-16-1863 (1-10-1864)
Warfield, Henry to Merica Terril 12-13-1846
Warmack, S. B. to N. Catherine Heatherley 5-6-1870 (5-12-1870)
Warner, Wm. H. H. to Nancy E. Lay 6-13-1858
Waters, Aaron D. to Emeline Parrott 5-20-1855 (no return)
Waters, Champ to Nelly McMunn 3-16-1843 (no return)
Waters, Champless to Nelly McMinn 3-16-1843 (3-21-1843)
Waters, Joseph to Mary E. Tiller 10-16-1873
Waters, Samuel to Lydia Roberts 3-8-1850
Watkins, Beverly to Alphaomega Watts 7-6-1875
Watson, William to Lucinday Day 10-31-1838 (no return)
Watson?, James to Manda Miller 1-6-1880 (1-7-1880)
Weaver, Calvin to Elizabeth Myers 1-13-1858
Weaver, Daniel to Elizabeth Norris 11-11-1861 (11-16-1861)
Weaver, Jacob to Eliza Baily 10-18-1871 (10-19-1871)
Weaver, N. P. to Eliza A. Reeves 1-14-1853 (1-16-1853)
Weaver, Thomas to Seloma C. Shown 11-27-1872 (11-28-1872)
Webb, Abraham H. to F. Lankford 11-3-1871
Webb, George W. to Martha Polston 12-30-1872 (12-31-1872)
Webb, George to Lyia? Griffey 11-15-1853 (11-16-1853)
Webb, James R. to Eliza J. Hays 1-11-1857
Webb, John R. to A. F. Reynolds 9-8-1876
Webb, John to Mollie A. Ordens 2-6-1872
Webb, Pardell to Louiza Wilson 8-14-1873 (8-16-1873)
Webb, Thomas to Nancy A. Brooks 11-29-1855
Webb, Wm. to Loucinda Dabney 8-15-1859 (8-17-1859)
Webb, Wm. to R M. Lewellen 1-4-1879 (1-5-1879)
Welch, Levi to Sarah Winerford German 1-31-1873
Welch, Sterling to Carmele Wilson 7-7-1877 (7-8-1877)
Wells, Charles W. to Mary E. Sharp 10-18-1869
Wells, Chas. to Roda Lay 2-24-1877 (2-27-1877)
Wells, E. F. to S. F. Bratcher 10-2-1876 (10-12-1876)
Wells, Elijah to A. Sweat 7-18-1878 (7-19-1878)
Wells, James A. to Eddy Fox 9-14-1854
Wells, James M. to Sarah Cooper 2-25-1856
Wells, Squire to Nancy Bratcher 11-3-1879 (11-6-1879)

Wells, Wm. N. to Mary Fox 8-17-1856
Wells, Wm. to Nancy Faulkner 1-1-1843
Weloby, James B. to Rachal Andrews 12-9-1868 (12-10-1868)
West, James H. to Elizabeth Campbell 3-6-1845
Wheeler, David H. to Elizabeth A. Sharp 9-3-1873 (9-4-1873)
Wheeler, H. L. to T. A. Hunter 12-22-1870
Wheeler, Henry to Ann Agee 12-20-1840 (no return)
Wheeler, Jack to Jane Gibson 4-16-1874
Wheeler, John R. to Amanda L. Smith 6-15-1854 (no return)
Wheeler, M. D. to Sarah E. Hunter 10-3-1866 (10-5-1865)
Wheeler, R. D. to Lucy Sharp 9-27-1880
White, Isaac to Lavina Sneaton 6-20-1846 (7-2-1846)
White, James to Eliz. Boruff 1-12-1856 (no return)
White, Steven to Mary Nickerson 1-28-1856
White, T. G.? to Annettie Bibb 7-8-1868
White, Thos. G. to Annettie Bibb 7-8-1868 (7-9-1868)
Whiten, George to Mary Ridenour 12-18-1864 (no return)
Whitenburge, J. W. to Malinda Todd 4-16-1877
Whitton, James R. to Martha J. Mazingo 12-24-1880
Wier, Joseph W. to Eliza J. Queener 2-23-1871
Wier, Sneed to Eliza Queener 5-14-1874
Wier, Sneed to Louisa Langum 11-9-1872 (11-10-1872)
Wierick, Jeferson to Margaret Miller 5-2-1873
Wilborn, Elihu to Isabell Walden 12-18-1858
Wilborn, Jas. to Loucinda Bolton 2-3-1859
Wild, John to Elizabeth Hinson 12-22-1851 (1-22-1851?)
Wilder, Joel to Malinda Holder 8-13-1876
Wiles, Levi to Mary L. Miller 5-16-1838 (5-31-1838)
Wilhite, Andrew to Nancy Stanlya 9-10-1855
Wilhite, Ben. to Elmina Edwards 12-23-1844 (12-26-1844)
Wilhite, Franklin to Lowry Leach 3-25-1864 (3-27-1864)
Wilhite, Jesse to Elizabeth Cox 11-22-1846
Wilhite, John Wily to Catherine Carter 2-1-1842
Wilhite, John to Mary Brock 12-20-1869
Wilhite, L. N. to M. M. Waters 3-20-1880 (3-21-1880)
Wilhite, S. D. to E. S. Elkins 6-5-1850 (6-9-1850)
Wilhite, Sterns to Catharine Carter 1-29-1843
Wilhoit, James to Manda Fonden 11-17-1875 (11-18-1875)
Wilhoit, Rufus to Sarah Tidwell 11-9-1875 (11-11-1875)
Wilhoite, Joseph to Dicy Wilhoite 7-23-1873
Wilkerson, James H. to Julie Anna Hubbord 4-11-1874 (4-12-1874)
Willhite, Ezekiel to Rebecca Grant 8-12-1852 (8-17-1852)
Willhite, Joseph to Isabell Tucker 1-20-1858
Willhite, Squire to Desa A. Massengale 1-23-1860
Williams, Adam to Mary Petree 11-8-1880

Williams, Alfred to Matilda Hutson 3-7-1852 (3-11-1852)
Williams, Calvin to China Niche!son 11-4-1865
Williams, Calvin to Jula Williams 3-3-1878
Williams, Elijah to Elizabeth Orice 12-1-1859
Williams, Govel to Margarett Siler 6-13-1841
Williams, Granville to Semantha Jane Evans 11-30-1865
Williams, Isaac to America Nix 8-19-1855
Williams, James to Charlotte Barbee 8-22-1845 (8-27-1845)
Williams, James to Mary A. Lovitt 8-20-1873
Williams, John to Nancy Thomas 1-10-1865 (1-12-1865)
Williams, Joseph to Catharine Petree 5-23-1855 (5-24-1855)
Williams, Peter to Sumess Sharp 2-12-1876
Williams, Robirds to Mary L. Shown 3-17-1870
Williams, Russell! to Mary Burnett 8-3-1838 (8-5-1838)
Williams, Silas to Catherine Smith 7-22-1842 (no return)
Williams, T. E. to M. M. Lawson 3-15-1880
Williams, William to Martha Sharp 11-11-1846 (11-12-1846)
Williams, William to Nancy Jane Tow 9-3-1880
Williams, William to Phebe Herron 9-24-1848
Williams, Wm. H. to Pricila Newport 8-26-1840 (no return)
Williamson, Albert to Louisa T. Brantlett 10-5-1840 (10-8-1840)
Williamson, Charles to Sarah Green 11-11-1850 (11-15-1850)
Williamson, Charles to Sarah Green 11-11-1850 (no return)
Williamson, J. M. to E. Nelson 1-9-1878 (1-10-1878)
Williamson, J. M. to M. E. Page 11-28-1863 (12-2-1863)
Williamson, Richard to Mary Thomaos 12-1-1881
Willis, David to Elizabeth Canter 3-22-1838
Willoby, John to Catharine Vanderpool 1-3-1844 (1-7-1844)
Willoughby, Elbert to Mandy Romines 1-16-1862 (1-24-1862)
Willoughby, Joseph to Rhoda Heatherly 11-20-1847 (11-21-1847)
Willoughby, P. to Martha A. Smith 6-26-1865 (6-29-1865)
Willoughby, Preston to Kesiah Hutson 9-5-1879 (9-6-1879)
Willoughby, Wm. to Cyntha J. Spangler 9-25-1872 (9-26-1872)
Wills, Lewis to Sarah Kincaide 6-16-1873
Willson, Samuel to C. Ellison 11-11-1855
Willson, Wm. to Sarah Leach 11-14-1858
Willsons, John E. to Hannah Smith 4-23-1849 (4-25-1849)
Wiloby, G. W. to Martha Rogers 4-6-1878 (4-7-1878)
Wilson, Abe to Louisa Curnutt 3-1-1877 (3-18-1877)
Wilson, Alfred to Sary Jane Robins 2-12-1864 (no return)
Wilson, Alplesent Council to Alcinda Penington 4-20-1870
Wilson, Andrew to Sephrona Chittwood 4-21-1849
Wilson, Calvin to Nancy Branum 11-14-1854 (11-16-1854)
Wilson, Calvin to Phoeba Housley 10-3-1863 (10-4-1863)
Wilson, Claiborn to Manerva Wilson 1-25-1870 (1-26-1870)

Wilson, Daniel E. to Eliza Cox 2-6-1850 (no return)
Wilson, Daniel to Sarah Gibbs 12-30-1879
Wilson, Edward to Hulda Cooper 1-20-1841 (no return)
Wilson, Elbert H. to Nancy Jane Jarman 11-30-1868
Wilson, Elvin to Lurana Boshears 10-23-1877 (10-24-1877)
Wilson, Enos to Sarah B. Knight 7-19-1870 (7-20-1870)
Wilson, G. W. to Mary Smith 11-11-1863
Wilson, G. W. to Rebecca Reed 1-6-1864 (1-7-1864)
Wilson, G.? W. to Malinda Robbins 5-9-1868 (no return)
Wilson, Hamilton to Matilda Siler 9-2-1850 (no return)
Wilson, Henry S. to Elizabeth Hously 12-9-1848 (12-15-1848)
Wilson, Henry S. to Nancy Catherine Wilson 3-4-1871 (3-5-1871)
Wilson, Henry to Jane Chavis 11-11-1859
Wilson, Henry to Sarah Campbell 3-18-1843
Wilson, Isaac to M. E. Johnson 1-6-1864 (no return)
Wilson, Isaac to Nancy Douglasls 7-17-1876
Wilson, James Edward to Amada? Jane Wilson 10-22-1870
Wilson, James H. to Louisa J. Lynch 5-6-1875 (5-7-1875)
Wilson, James H. to Lucy Ann McClain 9-2-1869
Wilson, James to Levina Phillips 11-2-1874 (11-15-1874)
Wilson, James to Lotty J. Reed 1-16-1864 (1-19-1864)
Wilson, James to Martha Agee 8-10-1839 (no return)
Wilson, James to Mary Hamlin 10-4-1850
Wilson, James to Sinty L. Veach 3-11-1880
Wilson, Jeremiah to Elizabeth Cox 3-28-1872 (3-29-1872)
Wilson, Jesse to Sarah J. Bullock 2-7-1879 (2-13-1879)
Wilson, Jessee to M. J. Dabney 9-4-1871 (9-5-1871)
Wilson, Jessee to Peggy McAmy 3-11-1847 (3-14-1847)
Wilson, Jno. to Julia Craig 12-3-1877 (12-9-1877)
Wilson, John A. to Rebecca Parer 11-19-1859
Wilson, John to Elizabeth Walker 8-20-1853 (no return)
Wilson, John to Emeline Luster 10-16-1876
Wilson, John to Frances B. Jackson 8-31-1846 (9-10-1846)
Wilson, John to M. Davis 10-28-1877
Wilson, John to Mary Adkins 1-10-1876
Wilson, Joshua to Jane Creekmore 12-12-1841
Wilson, Lewis G. to Amanda E. Yount 3-25-1871
Wilson, Lewis to Elisa J. Wilson 12-21-1878 (12-23-1878)
Wilson, Lewis to Elizabeth Hansly 9-24-1840? (no return)
Wilson, Lewis to Martha Vest 12-7-1867 (12-8-1867)
Wilson, Nelson to Martha Cloud 10-11-1855 (10-16-1855)
Wilson, Sampson to Elizabeth Parker 7-27-1853 (no return)
Wilson, Sampson to Mary Carroll 11-17-1879
Wilson, Samuel to Mary Hambliln 3-24-1881
Wilson, Shampson to Sarah Walker 9-22-1849 (10-4-1849)

Wilson, Thompson to Sarah Walker 9-22-1849 (no return)
Wilson, W. C. to Elisa Jarmon 8-25-1875
Wilson, W. R. to Sarah E. Webb 3-13-1879 (3-16-1879)
Wilson, William to Mariah Wilson 3-26-1845 (no return)
Wilson, William to Sarah Pitman 11-11-1840 (11-12-1840)
Wilson, William to Susan Adams 5-17-1868
Winton, J. C. to Louisa Richardson 8-25-1853 (8-26-1853)
Withers, Bushrod to Elizabeth Bratcher 4-16-1845 (94-17-1845)
Witt, Edmund to Lucinda Loy 11-1-1844 (11-3-1844)
Witt, Francis to Mary J. Stanly 2-3-1868 (3-6-1868)
Witt, Frank to Cintha Irwin 7-11-1868 (no return)
Witt, G. W. to Mary Jane Smith 2-17-1851 (no return)
Witt, Hiram to Sumer E. Moses 2-11-1881
Witt, John to Martha C. Sharp 11-4-1852 (11-7-1852)
Witt, John to Polly Snodderly 1-14-1847 (no return)
Witt, Washington to Mary Tow 5-26-1870
Witt, Washington to Rebecca Brown 10-15-1838 (no return)
Wombles, Robert to Malinda Cox 8-27-1864
Wood, C. to Elizabeth J. Keeney 5-6-1868 (5-10-1868)
Wood, Daniel to Mary Emely Keeney 9-16-1870 (9-18-1870)
Wood, Matison to Polley Reynolds 10-1-1880 (10-3-1880)
Wood, Wm. to Maggie Bound 6-12-1874 (6-13-1874)
Woods, A. B. to Maryann Anderson 9-2-1869
Woods, Henry to Ann Rice 9-12-1843 (9-14-1843)
Woods, Henry to Annis Housley 11-25-1871 (11-28-1871)
Woods, Horrace to Catherine Reynolds 10-22-1873
Woods, James to Eliza Smith 5-23-1872 (5-26-1872)
Woods, Joel to Hanah M. Pulium 3-11-1869
Woods, John to Mary Martin 4-15-1851
Woods, Nathanial to P. Elkins 1-21-1852
Woods; Pleasant W. to Susan Karr 7-1-1847
Woods, Simeon to Mary Clark 11-29-1855 (11-30-1855)
Woods, William to Maggie Bounds 6-12-1874
Woodson, Silas to Jane Miller 5-29-1858 (6-3-1858)
Woodward, C. M. to Lucy Hill 11-23-1878 (11-24-1878)
Woodward, John F. to Mary Wilson 1-2-1878
Woodward, Wm. to Leah Ford 10-4-1843 (10-8-1843)
Wright, David to Nancy Comer 2-26-1853 (no return)
Wright, H. H. to S. A. Shepard 2-20-1877 (3-11-1877)
Wright, J. R. to Jane Russell 10-28-1876
Wright, Robert to Elizabeth Riggs 1-22-1881
Wright, Wm. to Sarah Chapman 12-3-1850 (12-8-1850)
Wyatt, Milton to Nancy Ann Allison 3-15-1843
Wyrick, Thos. to Angeline Malicoat 11-6-1876 (11-8-1876)
Yager, Thos. J. to Artty? Bruce 9-27-1862

Yearee, C. J. to Margaret J. Ryan 4-10-1859
York, Andrew to Polly York 2-11-1865 (2-12-1865)
York, F. K. to P. K. Barham? 7-31-1879
York, John to Mary Ann Marlow 2-17-1881
York, Joseph to Nancy J. Marra 6-2-1859
York, Joseph to Rebecca Duncan 2-5-1841
York, Joseph to Sarah Crosswhite 1-4-1856
York, Martin to China York 8-27-1865
York, Thomas to Elizabeth Cruse 1-14-1855
York, Thomas to Sarah Johnson 12-8-1842
York, W. Allen to Nancy Jane Snodderley 1-9-1871
York, Williams to Martha Brock 3-19-1845 (3-20-1845)
York, Wm. to Lucretia J. Riggs 11-10-1876
York, Wm. to Rebecca Low 3-30-1868 (4-2-1868)
York, Wm. to Rebecca Williamls 4-28-1868
Young, C. J. to Vergina Laford 9-16-1869
Young, Ephraim to Rebecca Hutson 12-23-1854 (no return)
Young, Jo to Pernett Sexton 3-16-1878 (3-17-1878)
Young, John C. to Nancy Walker 9-13-1856
Young, Joseph to Martha A. Petitt 1-30-1864 (no return)
Young, Tho. to Loucinda McPeely 3-2-1859 (3-6-1859)
Young, Thomas to Artela Fox 6-25-1853
Yourk, James to Armelda Woolem 8-22-1870
Yourk, John to Herriet Woolen 8-22-1870
Yourk, Lewis to Amanda Yourk 8-22-1870

INDEX

TO

BRIDES

Abbet, Barbary 8
Abbett, Jane 64
Abner, Mary 22
Acres, Jane 17
Acres, Lucinda 16
Adams, Elizabeth 55
Adams, Susan 72
Adkins (or Stone), Emily 57
Adkins, Anna Benneett 38
Adkins, Catharine 1
Adkins, Catharine 16
Adkins, Cerena 58
Adkins, Christena 59
Adkins, Delila 36
Adkins, Dosee 32
Adkins, Drusy 36
Adkins, E. E. 1
Adkins, Eliza 32
Adkins, Elizabeth 12
Adkins, Elizabeth 6
Adkins, Elzira 1
Adkins, Elzira 57
Adkins, Emly J. 63
Adkins, Emoria 37
Adkins, Freely 37
Adkins, Hannah 53
Adkins, Izeally 1
Adkins, Jane 30
Adkins, Jane 66
Adkins, Josie 50
Adkins, Julia A. 1
Adkins, Manda 44
Adkins, Margaret 7
Adkins, Martha Ann 5
Adkins, Martha Jane 5
Adkins, Mary 71
Adkins, Mary J. 24
Adkins, Matilda 51
Adkins, Nancey 57
Adkins, Ollie 5
Adkins, Polly Ann 28
Adkins, Rebecca 29
Adkins, S. Malinda 46
Adkins, Salina 41
Adkins, Salitha 30

Adkins, Sally M. 5
Adkins, Sarah 20
Adkins, Sefroney 62
Adkins, Serelda 54
Adkins, Serepta S. 30
Adkins, Susannah 35
Agee, Ann 69
Agee, Anna 1
Agee, Elizabeth 14
Agee, Martha 71
Agee, Sallie 7
Albright, Louisa 11
Albright, Polly 45
Alder, America 8
Alder, Manervy 52
Alder, Mary E. 52
Alder, Sarah 64
Alenl, Elizabeth J. 58
Alison, Oliv P. 17
Allbright, Orpha 63
Alleln, Mary A. 3
Allen, Jane 18
Allen, Leurana 48
Allen, M. E. 19
Allen, M. E. 19
Allen, Mary 57
Allen, Nancy 26
Allison, Nancy Ann 72
Anderson, Elizabeth 28
Anderson, Elizabeth 36
Anderson, Louisa 38
Anderson, Margaret 52
Anderson, Margaret 54
Anderson, Maryann 72
Anderson, Nancy 55
Anderson, Nancy A. 45
Anderson, Relda 11
Andrews, N. A. 25
Andrews, Rachal 69
Angel, Eliza 34
Angel, M. A. 42
Angel, Nancey 34
Angel, Nancey J. 64
Angel, Permelia Ann 29
Angoner, Mary 61

Ann, Polly 65
Archer, Charlotta 22
Archer, Cintha 16
Archer, Jane 39
Archer, Louisa 39
Archer, Lucy 32
Archer, Nancey 62
Archer, Nancy 19
Armstrong, Elisabeth 37
Arther, Louisa 11
Arther, Nancy 62
Arton, Rebecca 63
Ashworth, Mary A. 23
Atkins, Emily J. 12
Ausmus, Vicy 64
Ayers, Catherine 38
Ayers, Florence 36
Ayers, Jane 53
Ayers, Laura 54
Ayers, M. L. 63
Ayers, Sarah 61
Ayres, Susan Emaline 7
Bailey, Elizabeth 54
Bailey, Martha 27
Bailey, Susan 7
Baily, Eliza 68
Baily, Eliza Jane 20
Baily, Elizabeth 33
Baily, Elizabeth 56
Baily, H. 38
Baily, L. A. 66
Baily, Polly 66
Baily, Rachel 64
Baird, Caney 19
Baird, Canney 4
Baird, Delila 22
Baird, Dianah 52
Baird, Elisabeth 48
Baird, Elizabeth 14
Baird, Elizabeth 18
Baird, Hanah 3
Baird, Hannah 19
Baird, M. J. 4
Baird, Mainda 26
Baird, Martha Jane 36

Baird, Nancy 35
Baird, Nancy 65
Baird, Rachel 36
Baird, Rachel 48
Baird, Rachel 48
Baird, Rebecca 9
Baird, Saphrona 25
Baird, Sinthey 45
Baird, Susan 54
Baird, Tacia 48
Baker, Bitha 8
Baker, Catherine 44
Baker, Kisiah 16
Baker, Lucy 50
Baker, Nancey 15
Baker, Nancey 60
Baker, Nancy 6
Baker, Orelena 66
Ball, Lucinda 19
Ball, M. E. 22
Ball, Polly 64
Ballard, Mary 54
Balton, Martha 67
Bane, Catharine 15
Barbee, Charlotte 70
Barber, Polley 58
Barbey, Hannah 62
Barbey, Nancy 18
Bardling, Emely 46
Barham?, P. K. 73
Barron, Conney 16
Barron, Flemon 16
Barron, Nancy 4
Barron, Nancy Emeline 57
Barron, Phebe 2
Barton, M. L. 28
Bashim?, Malinda 48
Bawl, Volentine 1
Baxter, Martha 62
Bayless, Sarah 25
Beams, Hannah 21
Beams, Jane 62
Beams, Nancy 16
Beams, Niche! 28
Beams, Rachael 27

Beams?, Anna 64
Beard, Hannah 62
Beard, Isbald 14
Beard, Lydia 36
Beard, Rachael 62
Bedkin, Sarah 25
Belelw, Elizabeth 35
Benet, Elizabeth 35
Benge, Jane 50
Benit, Nancy 25
Bennet, Lucinda 35
Bennet, M. J. 54
Bennett, Mary Jane 6
Bennett, Polley 5
Bennett, S. J. 44
Bennett, Sarah 25
Bennett, Susan 29
Bennett, Susan S. 59
Bibb, Annettie 69
Bibb, Annettie 69
Bibb, Josephine E. 67
Bibee, A. T. 29
Bird, C. J. 59
Bird, Caytharine 49
Bird, Lizy 31
Bird, Martha 1
Bird, Martha 13
Bird, Matilda 38
Bird, Nancy 39
Bird, Orlena 15
Black, Vicey 59
Blakely, Celerria 51
Blakely, Mary A. 49
Blakely, Nancy 5
Blakely, Sary 59
Blakely, Sisy 49
Blakley, Elizabeth 51
Blankenship, Nancey 54
Blankenship, Oly 21
Blevins, Martha 30
Blevins, Sarah 66
Blizard, Elisa J. 50
Boatright, Lavina 65
Bodkin, Emily 36
Bodkin, Melinda 65

Boid, Elizabeth 60
Bolen, Elizabeth 10
Bolen, Elizabeth 30
Bolten, Sally Ann 5
Bolton, Elizabeth 17
Bolton, Elizabeth Jane 1
Bolton, Emly 2
Bolton, Loucinda 69
Bolton, Lucy 6
Bolton, Malinda 3
Bolton, Margaret 59
Bolton, Mariah J. 9
Bonham, A. B. 63
Boot, America E. 56
Booth, Elizabeth 6
Booth, Lucy 48
Booth, Mary Ann 24
Bord, Syntha 6
Boriff, Titha 20
Boruff, Eliz. 69
Boruff, Mahaly 30
Boshears, Jennie 39
Boshears, Lurana 71
Boshears, Mary Angeline 30
Boshears, Sarah 65
Boulton, Elizabeth 56
Boulton, Martha 27
Boulton, Nancy 45
Boulton, Rebecca 32
Boulton, Susanah 2
Bound, Maggie 72
Bounds, Maggie 72
Bowline, Tobithy 43
Bowling, Elizabeth 31
Bowling, Iduma 62
Bowling, Louesa A. 24
Bowling, M. L. 18
Bowling, Volly 37
Bowlinger, Lucinda 32
Bowlinger, Ollive 49
Bowman, Caroline 3
Bowman, Jane 49
Bowman, Sarah 3
Boyd, M. J. 61
Boyd, Margaret 61

Boyers, Julian 20
Braden, Catharine 20
Braden, Martha 28
Braden, Mary M. 54
Braden, Sarah 10
Branam, Luiza 16
Branam, Nancy 30
Branama, Elizabeth 6
Branham, Eliza J. 55
Branham, Elizabeth 15
Branham, Nancey 62
Branham, Nancy 62
Brantlett, Louisa T. 70
Brantley, Sarah 54
Brantly, Nancy 50
Branum, Louisa 15
Branum, Nancy 70
Brassfield, Eliza 41
Bratcher, Cilly Ann 63
Bratcher, Elizabeth 39
Bratcher, Elizabeth 72
Bratcher, Ellen 62
Bratcher, Harriet 60
Bratcher, Mary 28
Bratcher, Nancy 68
Bratcher, S. F. 68
Bratcher, Sarah J. 40
Brathcer, Sarah 8
Bridgeman, Nancy 9
Bridges, Mary 43
Bridges, Sally 29
Bridgman, A. E. 9
Bridgman, E. J. 67
Bright, Elizabeth 52
Briton, Elizabeth 8
Brock, Cyntha 31
Brock, Martha 73
Brock, Mary 69
Brock, Surilda 31
Brockus, Thursey 19
Brogans, Lourany 55
Bronham, Lucinda 11
Brook, Frankey Jan 59
Brook, Susan A. 36
Brookes, Mahala 21

Brooks, Elizabeth 19
Brooks, Elizabeth A. 47
Brooks, Elizabeth Ann 47
Brooks, Lucy C. 48
Brooks, Nancy 21
Brooks, Nancy A. 68
Brooks, Nancy E. 11
Brooks, Siledia 47
Brooks, Sledia 47
Broos, Lucy J. 37
Brown, America 36
Brown, Catharine 45
Brown, Christina 63
Brown, Diana 43
Brown, E. J. 24
Brown, Eleanor 32
Brown, H. A. 42
Brown, Kitty 18
Brown, Manerva 46
Brown, Martha 29
Brown, Mary A. 24
Brown, Nancey 2
Brown, Nancy 66
Brown, Nelly 38
Brown, Peggy 67
Brown, Rebecca 72
Brown, Rosanah 21
Brown, Sarah 27
Brown, Sarah 38
Brown, Sarah 63
Brown, Vestia 6
Broyles, Catherine 62
Broyles, Cynthia 22
Broyles, Elizabeth 19
Broyles, Hanah 4
Broyles, Lucinda 62
Broyles, Mary 22
Broyles, Mary 65
Broyles, Nancy 26
Broyles, Nancy 65
Broyles, Nancy Catherine 3
Broyles, Nancy Jane 3
Broyles, Rachel 15
Broyles, Susan 4
Broyles, Susanah 15

Broyles, Synthia 60
Bruce, Artty? 72
Bruce, Elizabeth 46
Bruce, Harrieth 46
Bruce, Minerva 44
Bruce, Nancy 12
Bruce, Nancy 26
Bruce, Olive 52
Bruce, Permelia A. 12
Bruce, Sarah 14
Brumet, Mary 58
Brumet, Nancy 32
Bryant, Amelia J. 33
Bryant, Anna 51
Bryant, Candia 26
Bryant, Elizabeth 22
Bryant, Elizabeth 49
Bryant, Jemimah 29
Bryant, Martha 37
Bryant, Mary 1
Bryant, Nancy 47
Bryant, Sarah 25
Bryant, Selvana 7
Buckhanan, Caroline 38
Bullack, Lydia 49
Bulloch, Hannah 1
Bullock, Barbary 45
Bullock, E. 12
Bullock, Elizabeth Ann 26
Bullock, Lucinda 6
Bullock, Malinda 58
Bullock, Mary 30
Bullock, Mary 8
Bullock, Nancy 26
Bullock, Sarah J. 71
Bullock, Susan 26
Bunch, Jane 43
Bunch, Rutha 52
Burchill, Martha 47
Burge, Giney 33
Burk, Mary 10
Burke, Mary L. 2
Burnett, Mary 70
Burrass, Harriet 37
Burrass, Lucinda 13

Burrass, Martha 22
Burrass, Martha 22
Burress, Harriet 67
Burris, Eliza Jane 21
Burriss, Eliza 12
Burriss, Eliza 26
Burriss, Elizabeth 31
Burriss, Hannar 7
Burton, Ada 15
Burton, M. C. 27
Burton, Rebecca 15
Bustle, Mary F. 44
Butler, Edy J. 66
Butler, Eliza 18
Butler, Elvina 60
Butler, Manda M. 41
Butler, Meriah 46
Butler, Susan 13
Butram, Sousan 46
Byrd, Elzira 7
Byrge, Mary 10
Cader, Juli Ann 59
Cadle, Sarah A. 45
Cagle, Sarah 34
Caiin, Amanda 7
Cain, Ann 34
Cain, Frances E. 2
Cain, Hester Ann 40
Cain, Issa 18
Cain, Manerva 18
Cain, Martha 8
Cain, Mary E. 55
Cain, Nancy Y. 7
Cain, Pricey A. 44
Calahan, Barbara 21
Cambdin, Martha 64
Cambell, Elizabeth Ann 17
Cambell, Mary A. 42
Campbell, Catharine 56
Campbell, Elizabeth 46
Campbell, Elizabeth 5
Campbell, Elizabeth 69
Campbell, Jane 55
Campbell, Leah 19
Campbell, Lucinda 3

Campbell, Marino 28
Campbell, Nancy 22
Campbell, Rachel 58
Campbell, Sarah 71
Campbell, Susan J. 61
Canadya, Ozeda 18
Candy, Ceily 23
Cannon, Anna 8
Cannon, Polley 16
Cannon, Sarah E. 17
Canon, Nancy J. 7
Canter, Elizabeth 70
Cantrell, T. E. 13
Car, Luisa 12
Carey, Martha J. 26
Carey, Sue E. 17
Carnutt, Lucinda 32
Carr, Elisabeth 6
Carr, Lucinda 6
Carr, Rebecca A. 5
Carr, Vasta J. 42
Carrol, Mary 49
Carroll, Anna 42
Carroll, Catharine 23
Carroll, Celia 62
Carroll, Elisabeth 10
Carroll, Elisabeth 20
Carroll, Eliza 63
Carroll, Harriett E. 6
Carroll, Louisa 41
Carroll, Mary 71
Carroll, Mary Ann 30
Carroll, Nancy 9
Carroll, Sarah 24
Carroll, Sarah 40
Carrolle, Sarah 38
Carrot, Elizabeth 20
Carson, Margarett 6
Carson, Nancy 14
Carson, Polly 10
Carter, Catharine 69
Carter, Catherine 69
Carter, Eliza 19
Carver, Delila 26
Carver, Mattie 26

Carver, Nancy 9
Cary, Hellen 56
Casadad, Pheobe 24
Case, Ann 4
Case, M. D. 39
Caslin, Rhoda 21
Cates, Elizabeth 60
Cates, Martha 29
Cates, Mary 54
Caudle, S. Malissa 45
Caywood, Emly E. 55
Cears, Martha J. 66
Centres, Martha 9
Chadwell, Lyda 49
Chadwell, Mary 34
Chadwell, Mary A. 11
Chadwell, Mary Elizabeth 56
Chambers, E. 53
Chambers, Elizabeth 48
Chambers, Lucey 19
Chambers, Nancy 3
Chandrin, Eliza S. 51
Chapman, Ageline 36
Chapman, Calls 58
Chapman, Hester Ann 54
Chapman, Hesteran 14
Chapman, Leaner 47
Chapman, Lucinda 39
Chapman, Martha J. 61
Chapman, Mary Ann 55
Chapman, Mary E. 46
Chapman, Nancy 44
Chapman, Nancy J. 3
Chapman, Nancy J. 54
Chapman, Olivia 51
Chapman, Polly 60
Chapman, Sarah 72
Chapmana, Mary 42
Chatman, Emly 16
Chatman, Mary 26
Chavis, Jane 30
Chavis, Jane 71
Chavis, Sarah 30
Chavis, Susan 39
Cheek, Jane 49

Childers, Mary L. 34
Childres, Eaeley 62
Childress, Elizabeth 40
Childress, Lidda E. 27
Childress, Malissa 39
Chittwood, Eliza 38
Chittwood, Elizabeth 25
Chittwood, Sephrona 70
Chitwood, Patsey 52
Christian, Dosia 16
Cissle, Elizabeth 18
Claibaorn, Emma 51
Claiborn, L. V. 42
Claiborn, Love 47
Claiborne, Sousan 50
Claibourn, Mary (Miss) 35
Clark, Emmaline 38
Clark, Mary 72
Clark, Mary Jane 1
Clark, Nancey 22
Claxton, Bethena 16
Claxton, July A. 31
Claxton, Margaret 39
Claxton, Margaret 43
Clepper, Mary 21
Cliborn, Elizabeth 61
Clibourn, Emma J. 44
Clotfelter, Barbara 51
Clotfelter, Margaret Jane 51
Clotfelter, Mary 52
Cloud, Lucinda 27
Cloud, Martha 71
Coker, Elisa J. 37
Coldwell, Selvina 16
Cole, Nancy 4
Cole, Narcissa 48
Colins, Marthy C. 48
Collenls, Elizabeth 45
Collins, Cyntha 35
Collins, Rachael 16
Collins, Rebecca J. 62
Collins, Susan 39
Collins, Susan 39
Comer, Nancy 72
Comer, Sarah 29

Compton, Rachal A. 8
Condady, Mary R. 57
Conker, Polley 15
Conner, Melvina 12
Cook, Catharine 6
Cook, Tilitha 5
Cooper, Barbara 27
Cooper, Catherine 57
Cooper, Cathrine 50
Cooper, Elisabeth 24
Cooper, Elizabeth 14
Cooper, Elizabeth 59
Cooper, Hulda 71
Cooper, Huldah 37
Cooper, Jane 16
Cooper, Lucinda 6
Cooper, Mahala 32
Cooper, Martha 18
Cooper, Martha 53
Cooper, Martha W. 61
Cooper, Mary 14
Cooper, Mary 57
Cooper, Nancy E. 29
Cooper, Sarah 68
Cooper, Sophia 27
Cooper, Susan Rebecca 55
Cooper, Winnie 45
Corder, Mary 62
Cornelius, Susan 19
Corner, Catharine 23
Corner, Mary 1
Corta, Martha 10
Cotten, Elizlabeth W. 13
Cotten, Nancey W. 60
Cox, Anna 39
Cox, Eliza 41
Cox, Eliza 71
Cox, Elizabeth 69
Cox, Elizabeth 71
Cox, Jane 51
Cox, Julyatha 4
Cox, Lockey 61
Cox, Malinda 72
Cox, Mary 32
Cox, Mary A. 56

Cox, Mary F. 44
Cox, Nancy 52
Cox, Nancy 56
Cox, Nancy 67
Cox, Patsy 51
Cox, Phoeba 4
Cox, Sarah Ann 63
Cox, Susan 54
Cox, Tempy 39
Cox, Tilda Ann 54
Crabtree, Sally 16
Craig, Julia 71
Craig, Louisa 11
Craig, Lucinda 21
Craig, Nancy 32
Craig, Sarah 27
Craig, Sarah 55
Craig, Susan 65
Cravens, Lidda 23
Cravens, Saraha 58
Cravin, Elizabeth 64
Creekmore, Jane 56
Creekmore, Jane 71
Creekmore, Maryann 4
Creekmore, Nancy J. 19
Creekmore, Ruminty Jane 36
Creekmore, Sabry 43
Creekmore, Sarah 45
Crickmon, Cintha 42
Crickmore, Anna B. 48
Crickmore, Mary 42
Croley, Delila 36
Croley, Elisabeth Jane 40
Croley, Emeline 48
Croley, Jane 54
Croley, Malissa 55
Croley, Nancy 36
Croley, Phoeba 61
Croley, Rebecca 36
Croly, Elizabeth 25
Cross, Emily 1
Cross, Emily 17
Cross, Martha 47
Crosswhite, Ann 13
Crosswhite, Mary 43

Crosswhite, Sarah 73
Crowley, Ann 55
Cruse, Elizabeth 73
Cumins, Sarah 14
Cummins, Sarilda 22
Curnutt, Caroline 6
Curnutt, Catherine 44
Curnutt, Louisa 70
Curnutt, Lucinda 25
Curnutt, Milley 10
Curnutt, Nancy 42
Curnutt, Nancy J. 17
Curnutt, Polly 7
Dabney, Angletta 24
Dabney, F. M. 38
Dabney, Hannah 20
Dabney, Loucinda 68
Dabney, Louisa 54
Dabney, M. J. 71
Dabney, Sarah 22
Dabny, Alcy 52
Dabny, Elizabeteh 16
Dabny, Frances 30
Dagley, Katie 15
Dagley, Lucinda 54
Dagley, Mary 15
Dagley, Sarah 17
Dagly, Amanda 17
Dagly, Martha 3
Dagly, Mary 29
Dale, Ann Palina 5
Dandy, Elizabeth 5
David, Julia 59
David, Licey 30
Davis, Anna 63
Davis, Anna 64
Davis, Cally 62
Davis, Dolaphana? 45
Davis, Elender A. 64
Davis, Elizabeth 11
Davis, Emily 2
Davis, Esther 19
Davis, Gemima 52
Davis, J. M. 16
Davis, Lean 35

Davis, M. 71
Davis, M. A. 16
Davis, Margaret 4
Davis, Martha 52
Davis, Nancy 41
Davis, Nancy 43
Davis, Nancy K. 36
Davis, Polly 54
Davis, R. E. 28
Davis, Rachel 48
Davis, S. A. 48
Davis, Sarah 26
Davis, Sarah 51
Davis, Sarah 9
Davis, Sarah A. 48
Davis, Sarah Ann 65
Davis, Sarah M. 49
Davis, Susan 44
Davison, Rhoda 41
Dawes, Hanna 56
Day, Elizabeth 32
Day, L. C. 1
Day, Lucida C. 1
Day, Lucinday 68
Day, Mary 40
Day, Rebecca 54
Day, Sarah 47
Dayley, Nancy J. 54
Dean, Flourance 27
Dean, Mary 20
Deatherage, T. L. 35
Debley, Nancy 60
Delap, Rebecca 45
Delk, Didama 20
Delk, Mary Jane 37
Delk, Nancy 39
Delk, Nancy E. 8
Devemgill, Faitha 17
Dial, Elisabeth 4
Dial, Lucretia 25
Dial, Martha 36
Dial, Martha 56
Dial, Mary J. 30
Dial, Polly 52
Dike, Sarah J. 55

Dimerson?, Louisy 64
Disney, M. A. 10
Dixon, Jane 12
Dobson, Eliza 19
Doolan, Nancy 5
Dooly, Elizabeth 51
Dossett, Anna 66
Dossett, Betsy Jane 47
Dossett, Elisabeth J. 66
Dossett, Eliza H. 14
Dossett, Elizabeth 55
Dossett, Isophine 51
Dossett, Jane 65
Dossett, Manerva 59
Dossett, Martha 23
Dossett, Martha 49
Dossett, Mary Jane 13
Dossett, Melinda 59
Dossett, Nancy 14
Dossett, Nancy 3
Dossett, Nancy 31
Dossett, Nancy 41
Dossett, Nancy J. 8
Dossett, O. L 11
Dossett, Patsey 43
Dossett, Sarah 39
Dotson, Nancy 64
Dotson, Sarah C. 64
Dougger, Matilda E. 41
Dougherty, Clara 50
Dougherty, Crasy 49
Dougherty, E. 50
Dougherty, Rachel 57
Dougherty, Susan 50
Douglas, Jane 52
Douglas, Leah 4
Douglas, Lucinda 21
Douglas, M. 54
Douglas, Nancy Jane 3
Douglas, S. 61
Douglas, Sarah 9
Douglasls, Nancy 71
Douglass, Anna E. 65
Douglass, Catharine 22
Douglass, Elisabeth 11

Douglass, Elisabeth 48
Douglass, Eliza 30
Douglass, Elizabeth 67
Douglass, Elvina 8
Douglass, Louiza 48
Douglass, Margarett 48
Douglass, Mary 11
Douglass, Nancey 7
Douglass, Nancy 44
Douglass, Racheal 28
Douglass, Rachel 5
Douglass, Rhoda 9
Douglass, Rody 29
Douglass, Sarah 36
Dowel, Angeline 64
Dowell, Nancy 31
Dowell, Nancy 38
Draper, Mary Jane 64
Duke, Elizabeth Ann 5
Dunbare, Kitty 14
Duncain, Mary 29
Duncain, Sarah 11
Duncan, Eliza 9
Duncan, Henrietta 16
Duncan, Lucy 1
Duncan, Nancy 21
Duncan, Nancy Jane 2
Duncan, Rebecca 73
Dunken, Sarah E. 37
Dunn, Anna 39
Dunn, Catharine 62
Dunn, Rachel 14
Earley, Lucinda 52
Edwards, Elmina 69
Edwards, Manerva 51
Eldretlh, Marda? Jane 36
Eliott, Matilda J. 20
Elison, Julia 5
Elison, Roana 59
Elkins, E. S. 69
Elkins, Louisa 11
Elkins, Louisa 55
Elkins, P. 72
Elkins, Sarah Ann 32
Elkins, Surelda Bennett 22

Elkins, Susan 32
Elkins, Susan A. 32
Elliott, Ann 18
Elliott, Carline 56
Ellison, C. 70
Ellison, Celia Ann 32
Ellison, Eliza E. 21
Ellison, Josephine 41
Ellison, L. B. 33
Ellison, Rachel 59
Elsnick, Lucinda 55
Elswic, Nancey 2
Emery, Pattsy 12
Endle, Margret 2
England, Joanah 67
Ervin, Anna 40
Evans, Creesy 22
Evans, Elizabeth 33
Evans, Juda 41
Evans, Martha 17
Evans, Mary 24
Evans, N. E. 14
Evans, Sarah 20
Evans, Semantha Jane 70
Evins, Ellen 50
Farmer, Nancy 23
Faubus, Emily 64
Faulkener, Mary E. 63
Faulkner, Elizabeth 33
Faulkner, Elizabeth 58
Faulkner, M. 51
Faulkner, Martha 56
Faulkner, Martha J. 20
Faulkner, Marya 9
Faulkner, Melinda 46
Faulkner, Nancy 1
Faulkner, Nancy 51
Faulkner, Nancy 58
Faulkner, Nancy 69
Faulkner, Ruth 5
Faulkner, Susan 62
Fewston, Kisiah Ann 52
Flatford, Lucinda 46
Flatford, Mary Ann 8
Flatford, Mina 65

Flatford, Tyrena 35
Flemeing, Polly 24
Fleming, Sarah K. 10
Floid, Jane 64
Floid, Mary 52
Foby, Rachal 24
Foley, Jennie 66
Foley, Johannah 13
Foley, Sue J. 53
Fonden, Manda 69
Forbes, Leatha 66
Ford, Ann 21
Ford, Catharine 49
Ford, Catharine 53
Ford, Elisabeth 24
Ford, Leah 72
Ford, Martha 32
Ford, Martha 49
Ford, Mary 43
Ford, Melvina 12
Ford, Polly 31
Ford, Sallie 46
Ford, Sarah 20
Ford, Sarah 27
Forester, Alcey 28
Forester, Louisa 15
Forgeson, Rebecca 51
Forrester, Julia 32
Fortner, Susan 34
Foster, Polley 14
Foster, Rebecca 55
Fouse, Nancy 6
Foust, Catharian 8
Fox, Artela 73
Fox, Eddy 68
Fox, Elizabeth 29
Fox, Elizabeth 63
Fox, Hannah 47
Fox, Malinda 55
Fox, Martha 34
Fox, Mary 57
Fox, Mary 69
Fox, Prudy 18
Fox, Rachael 44
Frank, Mary Anna 39

Fraser, Sally 47
Fullington, Eliza 34
Fullington, M. J. 41
Fur, Vire 62
Gatlin, Elizabeth 40
Gayler, Barbary 37
Gayler, Elizabethe 3
Gayler, Martha 9
Gayler, Nancy 57
Gayler, Sarah 29
Gayler, Sarah 52
Gaylor, Elizabeth 67
Gaylor, Hanah 67
Gaylor, Hannah 30
Gaylor, Martha 22
Gaylor, Mary 15
Gaylor, Mary E. 19
Gaylor, Sarah 18
Gaylor, Susan 53
Gearman, Emeline 39
Gearman, Mary 22
Geaseland, Ann 57
Geaslin, Lucinda 56
Geesly, Winy 41
Gentry, Cyntha 39
German, Maranda 67
German, Mary A. 26
German, Sarah Winerford 68
Germin, Lavina 26
Gibbs, Sarah 71
Gibson, Catherine 54
Gibson, Emly 36
Gibson, Hannah 60
Gibson, Jane 69
Gibson, Martha J. 3
Gibson, Mary 41
Gibson, Nancy 22
Glander, Marida 28
Glandon, Clarissa 56
Glascoke, Polly 50
Glenn, Barbory 11
Glenn, Hester A. 37
Goin, Elizabeth 7
Goin, Martha 42
Goin, Mary 39

Goin, Mary Jane 44
Goin, Ollive 47
Goin, Rachael 48
Goin, Susan 30
Goins, Pheobea 23
Golden, Elizabeth 40
Golden, Mace 42
Goleher, Tabitha 14
Gooden, Manda 66
Goodin, E. D. 22
Gossage, Roda 42
Graham, Elizabeth 64
Graham, Laura N. 57
Graham, Martha E. 11
Grant, Abigal 9
Grant, Cynthia 17
Grant, has 36
Grant, M. R. 20
Grant, Martha 62
Grant, Mary 40
Grant, Rebecca 69
Grant, Thirey 36
Graves, Elizabeth 43
Graves, Martha A. 1
Graves, Mary 8
Graves, Rebecca 38
Graves, Sarah 11
Gray, Ann Eliza 53
Gray, Eliza F. 27
Gray, Elizabeth 54
Gray, Hannah 16
Gray, Isabella 31
Gray, Kisiah 37
Gray, Lydia 27
Gray, Manervy 53
Gray, Martha 53
Gray, Martha 66
Gray, Martha 7
Gray, Mary 53
Gray, Polly 10
Gray, Sarah 43
Greekmore, Elizabeth 41
Green, Elizabeth 5
Green, M. E. 37
Green, Mary Ann 49

Green, Nancy 10
Green, Sarah 70
Green, Sarah 70
Green, Sarah Ann 55
Green, Talitha E. 57
Greer, Jane 54
Greer, Rosanna 46
Griffet, Minerva 49
Griffey, Lyia? 68
Griffin, Harriet 21
Griffit, Frances C. 63
Grimes, Barbary 65
Gross, Angeletta 30
Gross, Hannah H. 24
Gross, J. C. 58
Gross, Kisiah 65
Gross, Kitty 8
Gross, Martha 12
Gross, Martha 30
Gross, Marthey 37
Gross, Polly 14
Gross, Sarah 46
Guan, Charlotty 56
Guffe, Elizabeth 67
Guinn, Nannie 3
Gwinn, Virginia C. 17
H. Lamare, N. C. 4
H. Queener, Mary A. 8
H. Walker, S. A. 28
Hackler, Delpha 61
Hackler, Elizabeth 5
Hackler, Rosannah 17
Hackter, Nancy 60
Haggard, Mary A. 45
Haggard, Mary Ann 45
Haggard, N. C. 23
Haggard, Susan O. 67
Hair, Mary 29
Hale, Eliza 13
Hale, Malisa 34
Hale, Nancy 48
Hale, Sarah 48
Haley, Pernelia 28
Haley, Polly 28
Hall, A. D. 33

Hall, Anna J. 13
Hall, Comfort 12
Hall, Mary 44
Hall, Permelia A. 39
Haly, Matilda 14
Hamblen, Feba L. 34
Hambliln, Mary 71
Hamblin, Keziah 6
Hamby, Rebecca 66
Hamby, S. J. 59
Hamilton, Nancy 36
Hamlin, Elisabeth 55
Hamlin, Mary 71
Hamlin, Nancy 16
Hamlin, Nancy 56
Hamling, Anjaline 41
Hammon, Mary 16
Hammonds, Mary Jane 3
Hampton, Anna 67
Hampton, Harriet 9
Hampton, M. T. 21
Hampton, Sarah 31
Hamptoon, Mary J. 39
Hancock, Rissiah 52
Hankins, Vilotty 10
Hansly, Elizabeth 71
Harding, Martha Emela 30
Harding, Sarah 28
Harman, Manerva 1
Harman, Mary 47
Harman, Sarah 14
Harmo, Delana 38
Harmon, Jane 4
Harmon, Jane 61
Harmon, Lucinda 38
Harmon, M. E. 27
Harmon, Martha J. 26
Harmon, Mary A. 47
Harmon, Nancy 18
Harmon, Nancy 55
Harmon, Nancy Jane 63
Harmon, Policy 22
Harmon, Polley 1
Harmon, Susannah 22
Harmon, Versula 18

Harnass, Lyda 23
Harness, Margarett 58
Harp, Delany 33
Harpe, Martha 11
Harris, Adaline 48
Harris, Helon 23
Harris, Leah 14
Harris, Lucinda 47
Harris, Patsy 25
Harrison, Lucinda 66
Hart, Polly 20
Hart, Telitha 30
Hatfield, Alphare 51
Hatfield, Amelia A. 56
Hatfield, America 67
Hatfield, Anna 32
Hatfield, Biddy 22
Hatfield, Biddy 64
Hatfield, Elizabeth 26
Hatfield, Elizabeth 9
Hatfield, Frances 17
Hatfield, Margaret 4
Hatfield, Polly 26
Hatfield, Polly 65
Hatherly, Mary 8
Hatherly, Nancy 18
Hatmaker, Barbara 10
Hatmaker, Barbara 3
Hatmaker, Betcy 10
Hatmaker, C. E. 16
Hatmaker, E. J. 32
Hatmaker, Elisa 27
Hatmaker, Elisa J. 14
Hatmaker, Eliza 45
Hatmaker, Eliza 45
Hatmaker, H. 2
Hatmaker, Hannah 14
Hatmaker, M. 15
Hatmaker, M. J. 57
Hatmaker, Martha 15
Hatmaker, Mary 54
Hatmaker, Mary Ann 67
Hatmaker, Mary J. 14
Hatmaker, N. A. 37
Hatmaker, Nancy 12

Hatmaker, Nicey 30
Hatmaker, Polly 26
Hatmaker, Sally 45
Hatmaker, Sarah 47
Hatmaker, Sarah 57
Hauskins, Martha J. 26
Hawkins, Margaret 25
Hays, Eliza J. 68
Haytes, Elizabeth 50
Heart, E. J. 63
Heath, Elizabeth 13
Heatherley, Alcy 19
Heatherley, Mary Ann 54
Heatherley, N. Catherine 68
Heatherley, Nancy 58
Heatherley, Temperance 43
Heatherly, Catharine 8
Heatherly, Catherine 29
Heatherly, Cathrine 29
Heatherly, Elizabeth 28
Heatherly, M. J 65
Heatherly, Marryann 54
Heatherly, Martha 14
Heatherly, Mary 25
Heatherly, Mary Ann 8
Heatherly, Rhoda 70
Heatherly, Sarelda 38
Heatherly, Serelda 36
Heathery, Luisa Jane 62
Heaton, Elizabeth 49
Helton, Mary 29
Helton, Mary 40
Helton, Sarena 40
Hembre, Margret 20
Henager, M. A. 59
Henderon, Catharine 2
Henderson, Martha 20
Henderson, Mary 46
Henderson, Mary 64
Henderson, Polly 63
Heninger, Sarah 27
Heninger, Sarah H. 61
Heninger, Sophia 3
Henson, Frances 1
Henson, Nancy 21

Heren, Olivia 13
Herren, Lyda 13
Herrin, Sarah 28
Herron, M. A. 62
Herron, Mary 21
Herron, Phebe 70
Heslope, Dolly 26
Hewett, Mary 26
Hewith, Clara 10
Hewitt, Elizabeth 25
Hewitt, Pheroba 1
Hibbard, Permelia 57
Hibbs, Haney 52
Hickey, Parmelia 53
Hickox, Mary C. 50
Hicks, Ama 5
Hicks, Easter 22
Hicks, Easter 59
Hicks, Elizabeth 50
Hicks, Elizabeth 59
Hicks, S. 43
Hicks, Sarah A. 4
Hicks, Susan 15
Hide, Lucy 26
Higgs, Mary 14
Higs, Elizabeth 6
Hill, Carley 14
Hill, Dealpha 32
Hill, Elizabeth 47
Hill, Endry 27
Hill, Lemuel 58
Hill, Levina 32
Hill, Lockey 7
Hill, Louisa 64
Hill, Lucy 72
Hill, Malinda 27
Hill, Margarett 46
Hill, Mary 42
Hill, Nettie 47
Hill, Parley 9
Hill, Permelia 8
Hill, Susan 61
Hill, Tinny 7
Hilton, Nancy 57
Hilton, Ruminta J. 7

Hinson, Elizabeth 69
Hix, Louisa 3
Hix, Malinda 17
Hix, Malinda 57
Hix, Rosey 62
Hix, Sarah 22
Hogan, Charity R 13
Holder, Malinda 69
Hollingsworth, E. 67
Hollingsworth, Emily M. 49
Hollingsworth, H. 40
Hollingsworth, Kitty Ann 56
Hollingsworth, M. W. 40
Hollingsworth, Martha J. 5
Holt, Amariah 46
Holt, Biddy 12
Holt, Elizabeth 35
Holt, Martha 59
Holt, Martha 59
Holt, Mary 36
Holt, Rachel 30
Honeycut, Catherine 9
Honeycutt, Cintha 6
Honeycutt, Mary A. 60
Hooper, Harriet 51
Hope, Eliza 18
Hope, Emily 51
Hope, Locke 16
Hope, Lucy 18
Hope, Martha T. 31
Hope, Mary 52
Hope, Mary E. 23
Hope, Sarah Ann 51
Hoper, Louisa 44
Housley, Annis 72
Housley, Caroline 32
Housley, Clary 21
Housley, Martha J. 7
Housley, Phebe 61
Housley, Phoeba 70
Hously, Elizabeth 71
Hously, Sally 24
Howel, Minerva J. 62
Hubbard, Elizabeth 31
Hubbard, Elizabeth 44

Hubbard, Julia Ann 15
Hubbard, M. J. 41
Hubbard, M. J. 41
Hubbord, Julie Anna 69
Hubord, Lucind 50
Huckabay, M. J. 27
Huckaby, Angeline 16
Huckaby, Eliza 26
Huckaby, Emely 43
Huckaby, Nancy 67
Huckeby, Martha Jane 4
Huckeby, N. J. 10
Huckeby, Selina 44
Huddleston, Jane 30
Huddleston, Mornin 56
Hudleston, Elizabeth 32
Hudleston, R. J. 49
Hudson, Elizabeth 33
Hudson, Louisa A. 48
Hudson, M. J. 53
Huff, Cynthia A. 33
Huff, Lavina 33
Huff, Leah 38
Hunt, Mary C. 46
Hunter, Alcy 55
Hunter, Julia 32
Hunter, Sarah E. 69
Hunter, T. A. 69
Hunter, Theresy J. 37
Huntsinger, Nancy 6
Hutsell, Anne? 58
Hutson, Catharine 55
Hutson, Elender 67
Hutson, Emily 65
Hutson, Fannie 1
Hutson, Jane 48
Hutson, Jennie 14
Hutson, Kesiah 70
Hutson, Louisa 28
Hutson, Martha 37
Hutson, Mary Jane 15
Hutson, Mary Jane 24
Hutson, Matilda 70
Hutson, N. J. 61
Hutson, Patsy 9

Hutson, Polly 14
Hutson, Pricilla 60
Hutson, Rebecca 73
Hutson, Sally 15
Hutson, Sarah 43
Hutson, Sarah 52
Hutson, Tabitha 45
Ingland, Feby 22
Ingle, Ann 21
Ingle, Elizabeth 39
Irvin, Jane 4
Irvin, Lucy 61
Irvin, Rachael 4
Irvin, Rachael 4
Irvin, Sarah 34
Irvin, Sarah 49
Irwin, Cintha 72
Irwine, E. J. 63
Irwine, Marya 63
Irwine, Sarah 60
Irwiwn, Orlena 63
Ivey, Armena E. 40
Ivey, Elizabeth 31
Ivey, Elizabethe 34
Ivey, Josephine 31
Ivey, Malinda C. 61
Ivey, Nancy J. 12
Ivey, Olley 31
Ivey, Rachal 7
Ivey, Sarah 23
Ivins, Amy 13
Ivy, Eliza 31
Ivy, Margeret 21
Ivy, Patsy 41
Izley, Susan 56
Izley, Susan E. 56
J. Bowlen, A. M. 24
J. Gross, Elizabeth D. 11
Jackson, Alcey 12
Jackson, Catherine 55
Jackson, Caytharnie 9
Jackson, Eliza 42
Jackson, Eliza 45
Jackson, Frances B. 71
Jackson, Martha 6

Jackson, Nancy J. 37
Jackson, Sarah 17
Jackson, Uva 51
Jackson, Vira 31
Jarman, Lavina 30
Jarman, Louisa 26
Jarman, Martha 26
Jarman, Nancy Jane 71
Jarmana, Polley 10
Jarmon, Elisa 72
Jeffers, Christina 15
Jeffers, Mary 38
John, America St. 50
John, Catharine St. 60
John, Martha St. 60
Johnson, Ailsy 52
Johnson, Elizabeth 32
Johnson, Elizabeth 33
Johnson, Elizabeth 4
Johnson, Emeline 9
Johnson, Jane 28
Johnson, Levina E. 32
Johnson, Lucinda 2
Johnson, M. E. 50
Johnson, M. E. 50
Johnson, M. E. 71
Johnson, Mary 38
Johnson, Mary A. 8
Johnson, Rebecca 23
Johnson, Reuhama 31
Johnson, Sarah 49
Johnson, Sarah 73
Johnson, Siothey C. 57
Johnson, Sousan 43
Johnson, Thursey Ann 31
Johnston, Lucinda J. 29
Jones, Delilah 33
Jones, Elisabeth 28
Jones, Elizabeth 20
Jones, Elizabeth 50
Jones, Elizabeth 58
Jones, Emiley 34
Jones, Emley 5
Jones, Harriet 55
Jones, Lucinda 51

Jones, Malinda 33
Jones, Martha 50
Jones, Minerva 28
Jones, N. W. 57
Jones, Nancey 48
Jones, Nancy 4
Jones, Olley 60
Jones, Rachael 21
Jones, Rachael 21
Jones, Rebecca E. 15
Jones, Sarah 23
Jones, Sarah 33
Jones, Sarah E. 2
Jones, Serrelda 25
Jones, Susan 6
Jordan, Margaret Druciller 14
Jordan, Margaret L. 16
Jordan, Martha 56
Jordan, Mary E. 32
Jordan, Sarah J. 15
Jordan, Susan Malindy 22
Jount, Rebecca 25
Jourdan, N. M. 32
Karr, Margaret 58
Karr, Susan 72
Kay, Matilda 39
Kecaide, Olivia E. 42
Keen, Mary 32
Keeney, Elizabeth J. 72
Keeney, Izabella 18
Keeney, Josephine 43
Keeney, Mary Emely 72
Keeny, Eliza 49
Keeny, Emerone 5
Keeny, Jane 8
Keeny, Lavina 6
Keeny, Nancy 17
Keith, Elisabeth 6
Keller, Elizabeth 27
Kelso, M. E. 61
Kelso, Sarah 31
Kelso, Sousan R. 25
Kelsoe, Elisabeth 18
Kenady, Elisabeth 40
Kenady, Mima 68

Kenedy, Elizabeth 40
Kennedy, Elizabeth 12
Kennedy, L. J. 33
Keso, Susan R. 25
Kesterson, Anna 59
Kesterson, Eliza J. 68
Kesterson, Lucinda 47
Kimberling, Matilda A. 42
Kimerin, Manda 23
Kincade, Sophia 60
Kincaid, E. S. 61
Kincaid, Hester 61
Kincaid, Heton L. 63
Kincaid, M. 67
Kincaid, M. J. 44
Kincaid, Mary Elizabeth 34
Kincaid, Minerva 58
Kincaid, Nancy 11
Kincaid, Nancy Y. 24
Kincaid, Nancy Y. 31
Kincaid, Olly M. 37
Kincaid, Pricillia 34
Kincaid, Sallie 46
Kincaid, Sarah 57
Kincaid, Sarah J. 58
Kincaide, Sarah 70
Kineard?, Martha 30
King, D. A. 23
King, Elizabeth 2
King, Jane 49
King, Polley 63
King, Sarah J. 65
King, Susannah 45
Kirk, Cola 42
Kirk, Coly 32
Kirk, Nancy 22
Kirkpatrick, Harriet M. 15
Kith?, Nancy 66
Kneedum, Elisabeth 20
Knight, Sarah B. 71
Kreckmore, Frances 42
L. Grissell, C. A. 30
Laford, Vergina 73
Lamar, Moss 1
Lamare, Mary 62

Lambert, Sarah 32
Lamdin, Margaret 64
Lamore, Susannah 2
Landon, Amanda 22
Landrum, Anna 22
Landrum, Betty 55
Lane, Rhoda C. 55
Langley, Rebecca 8
Langum, Louisa 69
Lankford, F. 68
large, Malvina 23
Large, Sarah A. 46
Lassly, Frances 60
Laugherty, Nancey 13
Lauson, Christena 41
Lavitt, Courtney 26
Lavzee, Nancy 24
Lawson, Ann 35
Lawson, Anna 55
Lawson, Biddy 9
Lawson, Elizabeth 10
Lawson, Elizabeth 43
Lawson, Emeline 22
Lawson, Louiza 64
Lawson, Lucinda J. 19
Lawson, M. 49
Lawson, M. M. 70
Lawson, Marget 10
Lawson, Mary 13
Lawson, Mary 5
Lawson, Mary 50
Lawson, Mary Ann 16
Lawson, Melind 41
Lawson, Milly 29
Lawson, N. G. 17
Lawson, Nancy 5
Lawson, Nancy 53
Lawson, Nancy 55
Lawson, Nancy 59
Lawson, Nancy 59
Lawson, Orlena 62
Lawson, Peggy 36
Lawson, Polly 53
Lawson, Rebecca 33
Lawson, Rebecca 40

Lawson, Serrepta 8
Lawson, Susan 38
Lawson, Zephry 60
Lay, Catherine 19
Lay, Catherine 3
Lay, Cawley 36
Lay, Celia 65
Lay, Cintha 62
Lay, Conny 36
Lay, Delila 4
Lay, E. S. 62
Lay, Elisabeth 17
Lay, Eliza Jane 3
Lay, Eliza Jane 58
Lay, Eliza Jane 60
Lay, Elizabeth 16
Lay, Elizabeth 21
Lay, Elizabeth 27
Lay, Elizabeth 49
Lay, Elizabeth 8
Lay, Emly 7
Lay, Emmaly 7
Lay, Hannah 3
Lay, Helen 23
Lay, Hester Ann 38
Lay, Jane 1
Lay, Leah 55
Lay, Levicy 8
Lay, Lucinda 60
Lay, Lucy A. 36
Lay, Manerva 16
Lay, Martha 57
Lay, Mary 16
Lay, Mary 3
Lay, Mary 36
Lay, Mary 50
Lay, Mary Jane 2
Lay, Nancy 19
Lay, Nancy 19
Lay, Nancy 37
Lay, Nancy 5
Lay, Nancy 62
Lay, Nancy E. 68
Lay, Rachel 1
Lay, Rachel 3

Lay, Rachel 48
Lay, Rebecca 22
Lay, Roda 68
Lay, Tarey 53
Lay, Winna 60
Lay, Winney 16
Lea, Nancy 2
Leach, Elisabeth 46
Leach, Jane 54
Leach, Lowry 69
Leach, M. E. 34
Leach, Martha 60
Leach, Martha A. 21
Leach, Mary Annaa 29
Leach, Mary Jane 59
Leach, Sarah 70
Leach, Susan 13
Leach, T. M. 10
Ledford, Mary Bell 67
Lee, Matilda J. 44
Lee, Sarah 35
LeForce, Malinda 5
Lett, Cintey 33
Lett, Louis 42
Lett, Martha 42
Lett, Melinda 29
Lett, Nancy 61
Lett, Sarah 55
Lewalen, Permeta 18
Lewellen, R M. 68
Ligo, Melinda 63
Lindamood, Malinda J. 37
Lindsay, M. E. 5
Lindsay, Mahulda 58
Lindsay, Margaret 38
Lindsay, Martha 37
Lindsay, Mary 53
Lindsay, Mary E. 24
Lindsay, Mary Jane 22
Lindsay, Theodocia 52
Lister, Voluntine 39
Little, Mary 20
Litton, Easter R. 33
Loe, Mary 30
Lofty, Parlena 39

Lofty, Sarah 50
Logan, Juda 27
Logan, Nerva Jane 38
Longman, Ann J. 10
Longmire, Barbary 43
Longmire, Louisa J. 57
Longmire, Lucretia 66
Longmire, M. C. 24
Longmire, Mahala 40
Longmire, Mahaley 45
Longmire, Nancy 53
Longmire, Nancy J. 53
Loops, Margarett 44
Los, Elizabeth 9
Losson, Elizabeth 25
Lovate, Susanah 9
Lovedy, Margarett 33
Lovely, Anna 33
Lovely, Elizabeth 38
Lovely, Kizzie 15
Lovely, Louisa 35
Lovely, Lydia 9
Lovely, Martha J. 35
Lovely, Mary Ann 65
Lovely, Nancy 37
Lovely, Telitha 12
Lovet, Cathrine 45
Lovet, Cotney 45
Lovet, Hester 19
Lovet, Loucitty 19
Lovet, Silvaniah A. 12
Lovet, Siotha? 25
Lovett, Frances 66
Lovett, Lucinda 17
Lovett, Ormela 42
Lovett, Sally 51
Lovett, Sarah 29
Lovitt, Mary A. 70
Lovitt, Mary J. 23
Lovley, N. 37
Low, E. 23
Low, Nancy 26
Low, Rachael 62
Low, Rebecca 73
Loy, Elisabeth 46

Loy, Elizabeth 23
Loy, Katherine 31
Loy, Lucinda 72
Loy, Netty 7
Loy, Sarah 56
Loyd, Metilda 19
Luallen, Polly 10
Luallen, Vicia 35
Lukes, Susan 28
Lumpkin, Bethina 20
Lumpkins, Ann 30
Lumpkins, Cath 47
Lumpkins, M. 13
Lumpkins, Tempy 27
Lumpkins, Tempy 56
Lunsford, Sarah 58
Luster, Emeline 71
Lynch, Elizabeth 8
Lynch, July A. 2
Lynch, Livinia 39
Lynch, Louisa J. 71
Lynch, Mary Jane 41
Lynch, Nancy 14
Lynch, Nancy 27
Lynch, Patsy 31
Lynch, Patty 47
Lynch, Pothe 25
Izby?, Martha Ann 29
Mackey, L J. 38
Macmand, Susasn 63
Madan, Mariah M. 1
Madden, Sarah A. 9
Madden, Sarah J. 32
Maddern, Jane 27
Maddin, Elizabeth 1
Maddin, Martha J. 2
Maddin, Sarah 24
Madors, Mary E. 63
Madren, Louisa 43
Madron, Mary 42
Mahan, Sarilda 5
Maize, Sarah 16
Malaly, A. 21
Malicoat, Angeline 72
Malicoat, Sarah 6

Malicote, Catharine 63
Malicote, Elizabeth 24
Malicote, Mary M. 37
Mallicoat, Francis 24
Mallicoat, Mary 38
Mallicoat, Polly 13
Maloby, Rachel 56
Malone, Arminta 18
Malone, Lucinda 66
Malone, Nancy 21
Manhollon, Nancy 7
Mapin, Cinthy Ann 9
Marcum, Lavenia 66
Marcum, Lyda 58
Marlon, Laphaney 33
Marlow, Catherine 47
Marlow, Catherine 47
Marlow, Elizabeth 50
Marlow, Hanah 41
Marlow, Martha 25
Marlow, Mary Ann 73
Marlow, Precy 18
Marlow, Susan 18
Marra, Nancy J. 73
Marrs, Lucinda H. 3
Marrs, S. C. 3
Mars, Martha J. 34
Marshall, Allice A. 29
Marshall, Mary Ann 40
Marshall, Nancy Ann 12
Martin, Elizabeth 1
Martin, Elizabeth 48
Martin, Lanya 52
Martin, Mariah 13
Martin, Mary 72
Martin, Rebecca 20
Martin, Sarah E. 48
Martin, Susan 50
Maser, Elisabeth 15
Masingal, Nancy 25
Masingo, Margaret A. 11
Massengale, Desa A. 69
Massengil, Eliza 34
Massingal, Cinthia 27
Massingal, Mary 2

Massingala, Sarah 16
Maupin, Love 2
Maupin, M. J. 52
Maupin, Margaret 59
Maupin, Maria 61
Maupin, Mary Jane 13
Maupin, Mary M. 60
Maupin, Nancy 51
Maupin, Sally 42
Maupin, Sarah 58
Maupin, Virginia C. 50
Mays, Elizabeth 48
Mays, Salena 56
Mays, Susan 40
Maze, July 51
Maze, Nancy 1
Mazingo, Elizabeth 22
Mazingo, Martha J. 69
Mazingoe, Elizabeth 21
McAmis, Louiza 40
McAmy, Peggy 71
McCall, L. R. 1
McCarta, Pelina Jane 1
McCarty, Elizabeth 53
McCarty, Frances 64
McCarty, Levina 43
McCarty, Martha 50
McCarty, Mary 64
McCarty, Melinda 28
McCarty, Phebe 39
McCay, Jane 36
McCidy, Elender 17
McClain, Lucy Ann 63
McClain, Lucy Ann 71
McClary, Susan 61
McCoy, Mary 9
McCoy, Milly Ann 61
McCullah, Sarah S. 35
McCulley, Elizabeth 12
McCulley, Elizabeth 22
McCulley, Sarah 43
McCully, Amanda 44
McCully, E. 31
McCully, M. A. 6
McCully, Martha 42

McCully, Nancy 43
McCully, Sally 58
McDonald, Finby 52
McDonald, Lucinda 38
McDonold, Nancy 17
McDy, Martha 15
McFall, Manday 63
McFarlalnd, Nancy 66
McFarland, Claris 52
McFarland, Elizabeth 4
McFarland, Elizabeth 59
McFarland, H. 56
McFarland, Jane 63
McFarland, Rachel E. 56
McFarland, Rebecca 34
McFarland, Rosanah 56
McFarland, Seta 54
McFarland, Susan 61
McGee, Isafana 47
McGee, Isey 40
McGee, M. E. 10
McGee, Manervey 68
McGee, Polley 10
McGhee, Juda 35
McGhee, Sally 33
McGlathlin, Elizabeth 42
McGlauthlin, Alcy 66
McGlothlin, Amanda 61
McGlothlin, Lucy 23
McGlothlin, Nancey 41
McGraw, Martha 47
McGraw, Sarah 4
McGraw, Sarah 58
McKamy, Polly Ann 68
McKee, Patsy 30
McKeehan, Nancy 21
McKeehan, Thursy Ann 16
McKehan, Catharine 23
McKidy, Chany 51
McKidy, M. J. 35
McKinis?, Nancy J. 26
McLain, Susan 7
McLane, Mary 43
McMinn, Nelly 68
McMunn, Nelly 68

McNeal, Eliza 7
McNeely, Lizzie 37
McNeely, Nancy 4
McNeely, Nancy J. 1
McNeely, Polly 61
McNew, Annah 43
McNew, Casandria 13
McNew, Catharine 60
McNew, Elizabeth 18
McNew, H. M. 11
McNew, Martha 31
McNew, Martha 50
McNew, Mattie L. 26
McNew, Minerva 31
McPeely, Loucinda 73
Mcully, Mary 31
Meaders, Lucey 13
Meaders, Lydia 18
Meador, Catharine 19
Meador, Jane 29
Meadors, Elizabeth 16
Meadors, Sarah 2
Meadors, Sarah 59
Meadow, Anna Martha 45
Medlock, Louisa 30
Melton, Allice 12
Mereda (Meridith), E. 26
Mergan, Hety Cathrine 4
Merida, E. J. 36
Meriday, Nancy V. 64
Meritt, Sarah M. 62
Mettinbarger, E. J. 48
Miles, Sarah 40
Miles, Sarah 52
Miller, Alice 43
Miller, Alseye 21
Miller, Caroline 23
Miller, Catharine 54
Miller, Catherine 35
Miller, Cathrine 18
Miller, Ceala A. 39
Miller, Celia 31
Miller, Celia 54
Miller, Eliza 57
Miller, Elizabeth 23

Miller, Elizabeth 33
Miller, Elizabeth 46
Miller, Elizabeth 7
Miller, Elizabeth 8
Miller, Elly Ann 6
Miller, Fillis 44
Miller, Hannah 62
Miller, Hulda 10
Miller, Irena 34
Miller, Jane 26
Miller, Jane 67
Miller, Jane 72
Miller, Julia 58
Miller, Lavina 9
Miller, Liddy 23
Miller, Louisa 62
Miller, Lucy 19
Miller, Manda 68
Miller, Margaret 40
Miller, Margaret 42
Miller, Margaret 47
Miller, Margaret 69
Miller, Margaret Ann 8
Miller, Martha 35
Miller, Martha 39
Miller, Martha 45
Miller, Mary 12
Miller, Mary 64
Miller, Mary Elizabeth 44
Miller, Mary J. 41
Miller, Mary Jane 28
Miller, Mary L. 4
Miller, Mary L. 69
Miller, Melitha 24
Miller, Nancy 5
Miller, Nancy 60
Miller, Rachel 11
Miller, Ruth 5
Miller, Sarah A. 37
Miller, Summerfield 59
Miller, Susan 25
Miller, Susan 29
Miller, Susan 60
Millican, Nancy 30
Milton, Elizabeth 5

Milton, Margaret 63
Milton, Nancy 58
Mink, Susanah 30
Moffort, Delilah 28
Monday, America 14
Monday, Hester Ann 50
Monday, Sarah J. 10
Monroe, Senetha 49
Montgomer, Clarissa 23
Moore, Lucinda 42
Moore, Mary 55
Moore, Mima 12
Moore, Polley 46
More, Almeda 26
Morgan, Holly 34
Morgan, Idea 35
Morgan, Manervey L. 12
Morgan, Mary E. 17
Morgan, Nancy 34
Morgan, Pheba Ann 17
Morgan, Rachael R. 9
Morgan, Rebecca 50
Morgan, Sarah Catherine 54
Morgana, Nancy 31
Morrow, Jane 60
Morrow, Mary E. 31
Morrow, Sarah 36
Moseer, Rachel 25
Moser, Elizabeth 14
Moser, July Ann 45
Moser, Mary 14
Moses, Louisa 10
Moses, Lucinda 10
Moses, Nancy J. 38
Moses, Sumer E. 72
Mosingo, Julia 11
Mouhollon, Elizabeth 10
Mowell, Uria 65
Mozier, Jane 67
Mozier, Nancy 10
Murray, Elizabeth 27
Murray, Elizabeth 36
Murray, Leah 19
Murray, Mandy 32
Murray, Martha 9

Murray, Mary 35
Murray, Mary 45
Murray, Mary Ann 12
Murray, Mary J. 25
Murray, Minty E. 56
Murray, Mornun 41
Murray, Rachal 58
Murray, Sarah 26
Murray, Susan 27
Murry, Lucinda 38
Murry, Milley 67
Muzingo, Catharine A. 13
Muzingo, Ellen 13
Muzingo, Hester Ann 41
Myers, Angeline 10
Myers, Ann 31
Myers, Brilly 34
Myers, Elizabeth 20
Myers, Elizabeth 68
Myers, Mariaha 63
Myers, Mary 34
Myers, Matailda M. 5
Myers, Melvina 57
Myers, Minerva J. 58
Myers, Sarah 26
Myers, Sarah E. 34
Myres, M. E. 34
Nance, Louisa Virginia 33
Nance, Mary M. 1
Nash, Sarah M. 54
Nash, Tilda 39
Neal, Ann 42
Neal, Elizabeth 57
Neal, Kisiah 60
Neal, Margaret 23
Neil, Lyia? 15
Neill, Martha 8
Nelson, Barbra 46
Nelson, Delila 8
Nelson, E. 70
Nelson, Mary 58
Nelson, Nancy 47
Nelson, P. 50
Nelson, Stena 11
Nelson, Susan 21

Nettles, Elizabeth 61
Newman, Martha 44
Newman, Sarah 8
Newport, M. J. 20
Newport, Pricila 70
Niche!son, China 70
Nicholson, Frances 36
Nickerson, Mary 69
Nickleson, Ester 33
Nilson, C. A. 11
Nix, America 70
Nix, Martha 9
Nix, Sarah Ann 51
Nix, Talitha J. 25
Norris, Elizabeth 68
Norris, Sarah 57
Norton, Adaline 61
Norton, Lucinda 62
Norton, Minerva J. 28
Nunn, Luviney 44
Oakes, Ann 28
Oaks, Leah 19
Oaks, Martha 12
Oatan, Matilda 41
Odell, Elizabeth 56
Ordens, Mollie A. 68
Orice, Elizabeth 70
Orice, Jane 9
Orice, Liddy 50
Orick, Mary 28
Orick, Susan 47
Orrick, Sarah 60
Osbourne, Elisabeth J. 51
Outen, Rebecca 31
Overbey, Louisa 42
Owen, Polly Ann 42
Owens, Armild 59
Owens, Elisabeth 23
Owens, Elizabeth 20
Owens, Harriet 49
Owens, Harriett 59
Owens, Jane 13
Owens, Julyan 60
Owens, Lucy O. 45
Owens, Mary J. 3

Owens, S. J. 7
Page, M. E. 70
Page, Susan 67
Pane, Elisabeth 65
Parer, Rebecca 71
Parker, Anna 43
Parker, Barbara 31
Parker, E. 17
Parker, Elizabeth 71
Parker, Elizlabeth 25
Parker, Esther 52
Parker, Julia 37
Parker, Levina 21
Parker, Lucy 23
Parker, Mary 38
Parker, Mary A. 46
Parker, Patsey 32
Parker, Sarah 29
Parrott, Emeline 68
Parsons, Liddy 28
Parsons, Nancy 48
Parter, Sophia 18
Parton, Jane 62
Parton, Mahala 45
Patison, Nancy 12
Patterson, Angeline 41
Patterson, Elisabeth 18
Patterson, Mary 33
Patterson, Polly 41
Patterson, Rachel 7
Pattersons, Mima 11
Paul, Angeline 37
Paul, Angeline 37
Paul, Mary 55
Paulson, Polley 43
Paulson, Sarah 43
Pawley, Rachel 19
Peace, Louisa 48
Peach, Elizabeth 5
Pearce, Margaret 39
Pearce, Mary 66
Pebley, Ann 12
Pebley, Martha 18
Pebly, Emily 31
Pebly, Mary J. 39

Pebly, Sally 40
Pebly, Tempy 31
Peerce, Susasn 6
Peetry, Susannah 51
Peirce, Mary 33
Penington, Alcinda 70
Penington, Rebeca 60
Pennington, Lydia 9
Pennington, M. J. 43
Pennington, Oma 34
Perins, Polly A. 19
Perkins, Cintha C. 48
Perkins, Cynthia 36
Perkins, Cynthia 5
Perkins, Elisabeth E. 51
Perkins, Eliza 11
Perkins, Elizabeth 11
Perkins, Elizabeth 45
Perkins, Elizabeth 6
Perkins, Elizabeth L. 53
Perkins, Jane 2
Perkins, Juli Ann 17
Perkins, Katy 24
Perkins, Kissiah 33
Perkins, Louisa J. 66
Perkins, Lucy 62
Perkins, Margaret 17
Perkins, Margret 27
Perkins, Martha 52
Perkins, Martha J. 66
Perkins, Mary 3
Perkins, Mary C. 8
Perkins, Mary Jane 28
Perkins, Nancey 4
Perkins, Nancy 34
Perkins, Nancy 35
Perkins, Nancy 45
Perkins, Nancy 5
Perkins, Permelia Ann 35
Perkins, Pollyann 36
Perkins, Rachel 22
Perkins, Sarah Matailda 24
Perkins, Susan 7
Perkins, Susan J. 61
Peterson, Mary 53

Peterson, Sarah 60
Petit, Adaline 59
Petit, Elizabeth 59
Petitt, Martha A. 73
Petree, Ann 21
Petree, Catharine 11
Petree, Catharine 70
Petree, Caytharine 49
Petree, Margaret 2
Petree, Margaret 58
Petree, Mary 69
Petree, Mary Love 63
Petree, Sallee 20
Petree, Sarah E. 2
Petry, Sarah 2
Pettett, Barbary 50
Philips, Elisabeth J. 14
Philips, Linton 14
Phillip, Elizabeth 30
Phillip, Nancy 17
Phillip, Sarah 10
Phillips, Arrena 67
Phillips, B. A. 59
Phillips, B. A. 68
Phillips, Catherine 5
Phillips, Clara 40
Phillips, Clara 68
Phillips, Clarisa 64
Phillips, Elizabeth 10
Phillips, Hannah 41
Phillips, Levina 71
Phillips, Lucretia 23
Phillips, Martha Jane 63
Phillips, Phebe 13
Phillips, Sally 8
Phillips, Sarah 8
Philllips, Lucretia 44
Pierce, Elizabeth 4
Pierce, Elizabeth 57
Pierce, Jane 42
Pierce, M. J. 41
Pierce, Martha 53
Pierce, Polly 42
Pike, Elizabeth Jane 54
Piles, Hannah 11

Pilkington, Joseph A. 40
Pinkleton, Jane 64
Pitman, Sarah 72
Plaster, Mahala 23
Pogue, Amah C. 22
Polley, Belinda 47
Polley, Elizabeth 55
Polly, Scinthia 65
Polston, Martha 68
Polston, Mary 58
Ponder, Malvina 67
Ponder, Margaret 28
Pondon, Margarett 28
Pope, Jane 37
Potter, Kisiah 65
Potter, Sarah 24
Powel, Elisabeth 23
Powers, A. C. 27
Powers, Charity 66
Powers, Elisabeth 47
Powers, Mary 48
Powers, Mary J. 13
Powers, Sarah 33
Powers, Sarah 6
Powers, Sarah Ann 25
Powoel, Catharine 55
Prater, Francis 21
Price, Pollyann 65
Prichard, Cordelia 21
Prichard, Molly 53
Prock, Metilda 38
Prock, Susan 66
Proffitt, Mary 37
Provence, Mary 6
Province, E#liza 13
Puckett, Martha 33
Pulium, Hanah M. 72
Purkapile, Ceila 37
Puteet, Duosy 33
Puteet, Jane 36
Putteet, Elizabeth 36
Pyle, Lucy 54
Pyle, Lucy 54
Qeener?, Susan M. 57
Queener, Catharine 11

Queener, Eliza 69
Queener, Eliza J. 69
Queener, Eliza Jane 61
Queener, Emily 44
Queener, Jas. 29
Queener, Josephene 51
Queener, Josephine 51
Queener, Louisa 48
Queener, M. 13
Queener, M. J. 21
Queener, Margaret 40
Queener, Margarett 61
Queener, Martha J. 27
Queener, Sarah 30
Queener, Tabitha M. 51
Quener, Julia 32
Quener, Olley 18
Ragan, Eleneory 62
Raines, Emely 37
Raines, Leuiza 66
Raines, Mary Ann 18
Raines, Timanda 2
Rains, Eliza 14
Rains, Elizabeth 10
Rains, Emily J. 31
Rains, Mary 33
Rains, Mary 46
Rains, Mindy 6
Rains, S. J. 1
Rains, Sarah 10
Rains, Sarah A. 10
Rains, Susan 52
Ralyaa, Elizabeth 36
Rawson, Sarah E. 12
Ray, Anna 3
Ray, Nancy 52
Read, Sarah Ann 60
Ready, Martha M. 51
Reagan, Sarah 40
Rector, Ardelo 63
Rector, China 33
Rector, Frances 52
Rector, Mary C. 58
Rector, Nancy E. 52
Redenour, Peny Ann 29

Reed, Cornelia E. 58
Reed, Lotty J. 71
Reed, Martha 61
Reed, Rebecca 41
Reed, Rebecca 71
Reed, Sarah 39
Reed, Sarah 65
Reede, Mary 43
Reeder, Nancy 59
Reeves, Biddy 5
Reeves, Cintha 67
Reeves, Cyntha 25
Reeves, Eliza A. 68
Reeves, Emeline M. 20
Reeves, Jane 29
Reeves, Luiza A. 20
Reeves, Martha J. 14
Reeves, Melinda 17
Reeves, Vicy 12
Resterson, Levina J. 14
Retherford, Hanah 47
Reynolds, A. F. 68
Reynolds, Catherine 72
Reynolds, Charlotte 20
Reynolds, Jane 15
Reynolds, Kisiah 12
Reynolds, Lucretia Bell 53
Reynolds, Lucy 61
Reynolds, Martha 65
Reynolds, Mary 35
Reynolds, Ollie 19
Reynolds, Polley 72
Reynolds, Roda 6
Reynolds, S. J. 10
Reynolds, Sarah 20
Reynolds, Susan 28
Rice, Ann 72
Rice, Elizabeth 31
Rice, M. J. 58
Rice, R. E. 51
Rice, Rebecca 22
Richardson, Catharine 50
Richardson, Caty 27
Richardson, Dicy 66
Richardson, Dicy 66

Richardson, Elisabeth 65
Richardson, Elizabeth 23
Richardson, Elizabeth 24
Richardson, Elizabeth 64
Richardson, L A. 26
Richardson, Lavina 67
Richardson, Louisa 72
Richardson, Louisa L. 57
Richardson, M. V. 61
Richardson, Manerva 53
Richardson, Martha 14
Richardson, Martha 34
Richardson, Martha J. 23
Richardson, Mary 67
Richardson, Mollie 11
Richardson, Obediance 42
Richardson, Rebecca 60
Richardson, Roda 64
Richardson, Sarah 39
Richardson, Sarah A. 26
Richardson, Susan 42
Richardson, Susanah 33
Richman, Susanah 29
Richmond, Matilda 55
Richmond, Metilda 5
Richmond, Nancy 5
Richmond, Sarah E. 24
Richmond, Saraha 48
Rickett, Juda 40
Rickett, Sarah 35
Ridener, M. E. 23
Ridenour, Cyntha E 25
Ridenour, E. J. 42
Ridenour, Elizabeth 43
Ridenour, Elizabeth 65
Ridenour, M. 65
Ridenour, Mary 69
Ridenour, N. J. 65
Ridinour, Malvinda 46
Riggs, Charity 10
Riggs, Charity 20
Riggs, Elizabeth 12
Riggs, Elizabeth 27
Riggs, Elizabeth 72
Riggs, Hannah 61

Riggs, Lucretia J. 73
Riggs, Lucy Ann 29
Riggs, Mary 65
Riggs, Mary A. 20
Riggs, Nancy 14
Riggs, Orpha 13
Riggs, Ruthey 54
Right, Eliza 41
Roach, Jane 2
Roach, M. J. 2
Roach, Margaret 7
Roach, Nancy 27
Roach, Nancy Jane 13
Roach, Rebecca 25
Roads, Emaline 51
Roads, Serreldia 2
Roaoch, Joannah 17
Robbins, Elisa 65
Robbins, Malinda 71
Roberts, Lydia 68
Robins, Elizabeth 26
Robins, Jane 21
Robins, Jane 45
Robins, Lucia 18
Robins, Martha 31
Robins, Sary Jane 70
Robinson, Docia 46
Robinson, Elisabeth 65
Robinson, Emily 54
Robinson, Jennie V. 7
Robinson, Martha Frances 7
Robinson, Polly 4
Robinson, Polly 52
Robison, S. C. 28
Rodgers, Mary 34
Roe, Nancy 19
Rogers, Agey 59
Rogers, Elizabeth 13
Rogers, Huldy J. 3
Rogers, Josephine 2
Rogers, Martha 70
Rogers, Mary 34
Rogers, Mary 9
Rogers, Mary Amanda 12
Rogers, Mary E. 42

Rogers, Rachael 36
Rogers, Sarah A. 7
Rogers, T. M. 37
Rogers, Tabitha 66
Roier, Mary A. 3
Roker, Ann 40
Roler, Elizabeth 35
Rollings, Catharine 56
Rollins, Mary A. 12
Rollins, Nancy C. 45
Romines, Jane 33
Romines, Mandy 70
Rooark, Caroline 64
Rookard, Fanny 11
Rookard, Mary Ann 50
Rookard, Matilda 52
Rose, Deily 67
Rose, Elizabeth 35
Rose, Jamatte 25
Rose, Jane 67
Rose, Litha 35
Rose, Mary 16
Rose, Mary 4
Rose, Nancy 35
Rose, Oley 55
Rose, Pheoba 3
Rose, Sarah 35
Rose, Sarah 35
Rose, Zephry 33
Rosier, Frances 52
Ross, Martha 17
Ross, Sephrony 13
Roush, Cela Ann 18
Row, Matilda 20
Row, Matilda 65
Row, Nancy 7
Rowlet, C. M. 65
Rozier, Jane 64
Rozier, Rachel 38
Runnels, Elizabeth 20
Runnels, Elizabeth 40
Russell, Elizabeth 11
Russell, Jane 72
Rutherford, Cinthe M. 16
Rutherford, Easter 67

Rutherford, Elander 2
Rutherford, Lucinda 53
Rutherford, Martha 6
Rutherford, Mary 3
Rutherford, Sarah 63
Ryan, Ann 49
Ryan, Margaret J. 73
Ryan, Melinda 63
Ryan, Rachael 3
Ryan, Sarah 64
S. Bow[ling, Mary J. 66
Sanders, Nancy 27
Sanders, Nancy 39
Sanders, Patty 56
Sandfill, Elizabeth 6
Sargent, Hellen J. 42
Saterfield, Barsheby 25
Sawyers, Susan 19
Sawyers, Susan 25
Sceans, Emily 46
Scears, Elizabeth 56
Scheues?, Mary 3
Scott, Harriot J. 20
Scritchfield, Anna 37
Scruggs, Lizzie 17
Seals, Susan 17
Sears, Sousan F. 25
Sego, Elizabeth 18
Seirs, Mary 58
Selvage, Elizabeth 6
Sentres, Rachel 17
Sequin, Aoral 39
Settle, Martha A. 35
Sexton, Arminda 49
Sexton, E. J. 28
Sexton, Leanner 50
Sexton, Marica E. 53
Sexton, Pernett 73
Sexton, Tennessee 68
Shadowen, Sarah 53
Sharp, Ann 43
Sharp, Arminta E. 25
Sharp, Avvey 16
Sharp, Barbara 57
Sharp, Catherine 11

Sharp, Eliza 61
Sharp, Elizabeth 18
Sharp, Elizabeth 26
Sharp, Elizabeth 26
Sharp, Elizabeth 37
Sharp, Elizabeth A. 69
Sharp, Hasy 29
Sharp, Jane 57
Sharp, Jane 63
Sharp, Lidia 44
Sharp, Linsey 19
Sharp, Louisa 20
Sharp, Lucy 69
Sharp, Lydia 27
Sharp, Mahala 15
Sharp, Margaret A. 53
Sharp, Martha 70
Sharp, Martha C. 72
Sharp, Martha J. 47
Sharp, Mary 45
Sharp, Mary 60
Sharp, Mary E. 68
Sharp, Mary J. 8
Sharp, Mary Jane 31
Sharp, Mary Martha 4
Sharp, Matilda 46
Sharp, Melinda 25
Sharp, Nancy 28
Sharp, Nancy 40
Sharp, Nancy 67
Sharp, Nancy C. 15
Sharp, Nancy J. 28
Sharp, Neley 57
Sharp, Nelly 15
Sharp, Parley S. 31
Sharp, Peany 26
Sharp, Polina 27
Sharp, Polly 20
Sharp, Polly 3
Sharp, Sally 63
Sharp, Sarah 19
Sharp, Sarah 27
Sharp, Sarah 32
Sharp, Sousan 2
Sharp, Sumess 70

Sharpa, Martha 2
Sharper, M. J. 27
Shelby, Frances 28
Shelby, Sarah 58
Sheley, Margaret 31
Shelton, Avy 44
Shelton, E. 1
Shelton, Jane 32
Shelton, Milley 53
Shelton, N. B. 43
Shelton, Susannah 49
Shepard, Rebecca 47
Shepard, S. A. 72
Shepherd, Ceila 66
Shepherd, Eliz. 34
Shepherd, Emily 46
Shepherd, Frances M. 43
Shepherd, Margaret 57
Shootman, Nancy 1
Shown, Mary L. 70
Shown, Seloma C. 68
Shumake, Cornelia 14
Silelr, Polly 49
Siler, Elizabeth 51
Siler, Ephy 66
Siler, Hester A. 61
Siler, Ireland 47
Siler, Julia 4
Siler, Lucinda 33
Siler, Lucinda 53
Siler, Margarett 70
Siler, Marilda 45
Siler, Mary E. 66
Siler, Mary Jane 58
Siler, Matilda 71
Siler, Nancy 59
Siler, Nancy 66
Siler, Nancy 9
Siler, Rachael 8
Siler, Sarah 39
Siler, Selatha 34
Silerl, Elizabeth 49
Siller, Damaris 27
Siller, Louisa 34
Siller, Susan 39

Skeans, Jane M. 63
Skeans, Sarah 46
Skeins, Emlie S. 24
Skiliner, Ann 60
Skinner, Jane 2
Skinner, Malinda 9
Skinner, Morning 47
Slatton, Milly 21
Slaven, Rebecca 64
Slier, Lucinda 35
Sloven, Caroline 27
Slover, Sarah J. 22
Smiddy, Anna Eliza 17
Smiddy, Elizabeth (Miss) 34
Smiddy, Elizabeth 35
Smiddy, Elizabeth 63
Smiddy, M. J. 33
Smiddy, Patsey Ann 3
Smiht, Judy Ann 20
Smimth, Martha 62
Smith, Alice 28
Smith, Amanda L. 69
Smith, Ann P. 7
Smith, Anna 49
Smith, Catharine 49
Smith, Catharine 67
Smith, Catherine 70
Smith, Darcus 52
Smith, Dicey M. 57
Smith, E. 66
Smith, Elisabeth 13
Smith, Eliza 72
Smith, Eliza Ann 29
Smith, Elizabeth 16
Smith, Elizabeth 19
Smith, Elizabeth 22
Smith, Elizabeth 23
Smith, Elizabeth 4
Smith, Elizabeth 40
Smith, Elizabeth 41
Smith, Elizabeth 54
Smith, Elizabeth 67
Smith, Elizabeth 67
Smith, Elizabeth J. 47
Smith, Emely 40

Smith, Emly 19
Smith, F. E. 12
Smith, Fannie 53
Smith, Flora T. 60
Smith, Hanah 35
Smith, Hannah 70
Smith, Helon 19
Smith, J. E. 58
Smith, Jane 51
Smith, Jane 60
Smith, Julia Ann 60
Smith, Lassia E. 63
Smith, Leanna 28
Smith, Louisa 3
Smith, Louisa 44
Smith, Louiza N. 42
Smith, Lucretia 61
Smith, Lurana E. 48
Smith, M. B. 18
Smith, Mahala 34
Smith, Mahaly 37
Smith, Margaret 25
Smith, Martha 35
Smith, Martha 7
Smith, Martha A. 70
Smith, Martha J. 18
Smith, Martha J. 66
Smith, Mary 13
Smith, Mary 18
Smith, Mary 30
Smith, Mary 52
Smith, Mary 71
Smith, Mary 8
Smith, Mary Ann 46
Smith, Mary Jane 72
Smith, Mary L. 47
Smith, Milly Ann 13
Smith, Minerva 29
Smith, Minerva 67
Smith, Nancy 11
Smith, Nancy 18
Smith, Nancy 29
Smith, Nancy 7
Smith, Nancy 7
Smith, Nancy 9

Smith, Nancy Ann 18
Smith, Pheba 23
Smith, Polley 34
Smith, Polly 46
Smith, Polly 57
Smith, Rebecca 25
Smith, Rhoda 58
Smith, Sarah 16
Smith, Sarah 23
Smith, Sarah 28
Smith, Sarah 31
Smith, Sarah 49
Smith, Sarah 57
Smith, Sarah 65
Smith, Sarah 8
Smith, Sarah E. 22
Smith, Susan 41
Smith, Susan 42
Smith, Susan 46
Smith, Susannah 9
Smith, Vicey 53
Smither, Eliza 1
Smither, Jane 26
Smithi, Elizabeth 66
Smithi, Mary 45
Smitih, M. D. 24
Smitih, Sally 5
Smmiddy, Louisa 29
Sneaton, Lavina 69
Snider, Malinda 21
Snider, Nancy 58
Snodderley, Nancy Jane 73
Snodderly, Anna 57
Snodderly, Polly 72
Snotherly, Elizabeth 3
Snyder, Elizabeth 59
Snyder, Mary 47
Snyder, Minerva 19
Soaps, Minerva Ann 23
Soaps, Nancy 43
Spangler, Cinthia 60
Spangler, Cyntha J. 70
Spangler, Evaline 42
Spangler, Evey Jane 64
Spangler, Nancy Jane 42

Spangler, S. E. 55
Sparks, Elizabeth 29
Sparks, Louisa 17
Sparks, Manervy 58
Sprowls, Louisa 7
Sprowls, Mary D. 11
Stanafill, Martha J. 38
Standle, Mary 56
Standle, Sabry 16
Standler, Sarah 9
Standley, Lucy A. 23
Standley, Rhoda 6
Standly, Sarah 52
Stanfill, Cintha 14
Stanfill, Cynthis 36
Stanfill, Elizabeth 22
Stanfill, Elizabeth 30
Stanfill, Hanah 3
Stanfill, Lucy 8
Stanfill, Margaret 24
Stanfill, Nancy 30
Stanfill, Nancy 35
Stanfill, Nannie 59
Stanfill, Polly Ann 59
Stanfill, Rachal 36
Stanfill, Rebecca 36
Stanfill, Rebecca 43
Stanfll, Cynthia 17
Stanford, Mary Jane 46
Stanly, Cintha 9
Stanly, Mary J. 72
Stanly, Sarah 1
Stanlya, Nancy 69
Stathem, Maggie E. 65
Steel, Eliza 12
Steel, Matilda 6
Stephans, Raganer 42
Stephens, Elisa E. 13
Stephens, Levina 45
Stephens, Margarett 45
Stephens, Margarett 7
Still, Gemima 50
Stokes, M. A. 21
Stokes, Mary 13
Stokes, Mary A. 15

Stokes, R. A. 10
Stokes, S. J. 21
Stoks, Mary Ann 37
Stout, Catherine? 18
Stout, Elizabeth 50
Stout, John 50
Stout, Louisa 46
Stout, Matilda 32
Stout, Nancy 2
Stout, Sally 38
Stout, Sarah 25
Stouto, Beubeca 29
Stowers, Martha 40
Strader, Esther 21
Strader, Martha 4
Stringer, Nancey F. 7
Sumers, S. C. 32
Sumers, Sarah C. 44
Suter, Josepine 59
Suter, Mary 12
Suter, Mary 17
Suter, Nancy 41
Sutherland, Mary 42
Sutton, Lulcinda 38
Sutton, M. U. 39
Sutton, Sarah 15
Swan, Harriett H. 8
Sweat, A. 68
Sweat, Elisabeth 64
Sweat, Frankey 57
Sweat, Lucy 20
Sweat, Mariah 32
Sweat, Mary 66
Sweat, Nancey 31
Sweat, Nancy 16
Sweat, Nancy 33
Sweat, Sarah 41
Sweaton, Jane 65
Sweaton, Rebecca 24
Sweaton, Sarah 33
Sweatt, Emely 60
Sweatt, Lucinda 34
Sweatt, Sarah 49
Sweet, Polly 59
Sylivan, Mary Jane 34

Tacaked, Rachael 65
Tacket, Nancy 2
Tacket, Rana 2
Tackett, E. J. 67
Tackett, Sousan 68
Talley, H. 34
Tally, Frances 10
Tally, Mary 23
Tary, Tiladay 12
Tate, Nancy 13
Tavy, Eady 29
Taylor, Caroline 54
Taylor, Elisabeth 19
Taylor, Eliza 37
Taylor, Evarilla 10
Taylor, Margaret 29
Taylor, Nancy E. 39
Taylor, Polley 37
Taylor, Sophia 7
Teagle, Emely 34
Teague, Martha 12
Teaster, Rebecca 50
Terril, Merica 68
Terry, Alcey 50
Terry, Ester 50
Terry, Rachael 61
Tetters, Elisabeth 57
Thomaos, Mary 70
Thomas, Catharine 5
Thomas, Catherine 30
Thomas, Elisabeth Cathrine 19
Thomas, Eliza 30
Thomas, Eliza 9
Thomas, Hannah 62
Thomas, Jane 24
Thomas, Jane 62
Thomas, Julia C. 24
Thomas, Lavina 9
Thomas, Martha 15
Thomas, Mary Ann 4
Thomas, Nancey 4
Thomas, Nancy 70
Thomas, Nancy E. 30
Thomas, Nancy M. 47
Thompson, Ann 60

Thompson, Carline 29
Thompson, Catharine 19
Thompson, Disa 48
Thompson, Elisabeth 44
Thompson, Eliza 54
Thompson, Emlie 24
Thompson, Hester 38
Thompson, Jane 35
Thompson, Jane 64
Thompson, Kiziah 2
Thompson, Mary 36
Thompson, Mary B. 32
Thompson, Mary S. 20
Thompson, Nancey 64
Thompson, Nancy 35
Thompson, Nancy 64
Thompson, Narcis 49
Thompson, Polly 13
Thompson, Polly 19
Thomson, Mary 28
Tibbs, B. C. 14
Tibbs, Elmira C. 26
Tidwell, Martha 56
Tidwell, Rachael 67
Tidwell, Sarah 69
Tiller, L. V. 66
Tiller, Mary E. 68
Tiller, Mary J. 45
Tillery, Ageline 11
Todd, Malinda 69
Todd, Melvina 64
Todd, Minerva Jane 56
Tow, Lucinda 2
Tow, Mary 72
Tow, Minerva 28
Tow, Nancy Jane 70
Trail, Catharine 10
Trail, Eliza J. 38
Trail, Elizabeth 38
Tramel, Bettie 41
Tramell, Louiza 51
Trammel, Deneygreen 3
Trammel, Mary 3
Trammel, Sally 3
Trammell, Dorcas 17

Trammell, Martha 57
Trammell, Mary 16
Trammell, Polley 56
Tucker, Isabell 69
Tuder, Martha 11
Turbinville, Amanda Jane 30
Turnbill, Mary C. 63
Turner, Anna J. 44
Turner, Liddy V. 67
Turner, Lucinda 10
Turner, Mary E. 44
Turner, Mary J. 48
Turner, Mattie 43
Turner, Susan 44
Turner, Susans 48
Turpine, Leny 28
Tuttle, Elizabeth 21
Tuttle, Mary 32
Tuttle, Mary 40
Tuttle, Mary 40
Tye, Elizabeth 32
Tye, F. V. 64
Tye, Frances 22
Tye, Margaret 1
Tye, Nancy 45
Tye, Thorse Ella 16
Vanderpool, Catharine 70
Vannoy, Timanda J. 20
Vatch, Lucy 62
Vaughn, Amelia J. 42
Veach, Nancy 53
Veach, Sinty L. 71
Veach, Thursay 54
Vest, Martha 71
Vilet, Martha J. 52
Vines, Sarah 4
Vinsant, Elizabeth 43
Vinsant, Mary 60
Vinsant, Rebecca 43
Vinsant, Sarah 24
Vinsant, Sousan 65
Violett, Martha Jane 41
Vittoe, Mary E. 25
Vowal, Lewesey 2
Walden, Delila 5

Walden, Elizabeth 26
Walden, Hannah 3
Walden, Hannah 45
Walden, Isabell 69
Walden, Jarelda 5
Walden, Nancy 57
Walden, Nancy 9
Walden, Permela 58
Walden, Stacy 45
Walden, Susan Armelly 2
Waldene, Martha 22
Walker, A. E. 55
Walker, Celia 8
Walker, Elizabeth 71
Walker, Eveline 51
Walker, Louisa 51
Walker, Louisa J. 34
Walker, Mary 67
Walker, Minerva J. 33
Walker, Nancy 73
Walker, Nancy A. 66
Walker, Sarah 71
Walker, Sarah 72
Walker, Sarah Ann 18
Walkup, K. 44
Wallace, E. J. 24
Wallace, Millie 27
Wallace, Nancy 57
Walton, A. J. 53
Walton, Sarah E. 33
Ward, B. 49
Ward, Elizabeth 11
Ward, Lucy B. 66
Ward, Mary A. 11
Ward, Mary Jane 11
Ward, Nancy Jane 68
Warner, Louisa J. 2
Waters, M. M. 69
Waters, Melinda 63
Watson, Elisabeth 56
Watts, Alphaomega 68
Weaver, Alcey 25
Weaver, Elizabeth 15
Weaver, Melinda 30
Web, Sarah 4

Webb, Delana 24
Webb, Elizabeth 53
Webb, Hanner 59
Webb, M. E. 68
Webb, Sarah E. 72
Weever, Hazy 65
Welch, Jennettie 15
Welch, Mary 43
Wells, E. E. 41
Wells, Eliza 46
Wells, Elvina 46
Wells, Malinda 49
Wells, Martha J. 24
Wells, Sarah 64
West, Winney 65
Whaley, Emmia 4
Wheeler, Anna Eliza 55
Wheeler, Bell E. 67
Wheeler, Clarinda 33
Wheeler, Nancy 39
Wheeler, Penelope Ann 56
Whitaker, Malinda 44
White, Aney 5
White, Lousinda 61
Whitecotten, Nancy Jane 24
Whitecotton, Lavina 46
Whitecotton, S. 55
Whiten, Sarah 1
Whitman, Kesiah 46
Wier, Ann 4
Wieric, Haney Jane 11
Wiet, Rebecca 48
Wilburn, Mary Ann 7
Wildrige, Lewerety? 29
Wiley, Sarah Ann 43
Wilhite, Elizabeth 17
Wilhite, Lucretia 19
Wilhite, Martha 13
Wilhite, Mary 49
Wilhite, Orlena 63
Wilhite, Polley 53
Wilhite, Sarah 46
Wilhite, Susan 67
Wilhite, Tabitha 35
Wilhoite, Dicy 69

Wilhoite, Polly 6
Willburn, Morning 12
William, Matilda 44
Williamis, Mary A.a 47
Williamls, Rebecca 73
Williams, Ann 38
Williams, Cena 55
Williams, Elizabeth 50
Williams, Elzira 55
Williams, Emily 55
Williams, Jula 70
Williams, Lucinda 44
Williams, Mariam 45
Williams, Martha 44
Williams, Martha J. 49
Williams, Mary 41
Williams, Mary 47
Williams, Mary 56
Williams, Nancy 28
Williams, Sarah 53
Williams, Susaner 44
Williamson, Margarett 62
Williamson, Martha 35
Williamson, Mary 21
Williamson, Richard 65
Williamson, Sally 66
Williamson, Sarah 33
Willoughby, Parlee 55
Willson, Nancy 53
Willson, Nancy J. 40
Willson, Rebecca 48
Wiloughby, M. J. 31
Wiloughby, Martha Ann 18
Wilson, Amada? Jane 71
Wilson, Angline 17
Wilson, Barbra 46
Wilson, C. 54
Wilson, C. C. 15
Wilson, Carmele 68
Wilson, Catherine 6
Wilson, Ceny 53
Wilson, Christina 38
Wilson, E.J. 20
Wilson, Elisa J. 71
Wilson, Elizabeth 18

Wilson, Elizabeth 25
Wilson, Elizabeth 7
Wilson, Emily 15
Wilson, Flora 10
Wilson, J. 65
Wilson, Jane 23
Wilson, K. 9
Wilson, Loraney 47
Wilson, Lorany 47
Wilson, Louiza 68
Wilson, Lurany 2
Wilson, M. 13
Wilson, M. 35
Wilson, M. A. 40
Wilson, M. K. 54
Wilson, Mahaly 32
Wilson, Manda 15
Wilson, Manda 38
Wilson, Manerva 70
Wilson, Mariah 72
Wilson, Martha 15
Wilson, Martha 58
Wilson, Mary 15
Wilson, Mary 40
Wilson, Mary 40
Wilson, Mary 52
Wilson, Mary 53
Wilson, Mary 72
Wilson, Mary Ann 6
Wilson, Mary J. 24
Wilson, Mary Jane 24
Wilson, Matilda 53
Wilson, Melinda 7
Wilson, Melissa 48
Wilson, N. J. 4
Wilson, Nancy 24
Wilson, Nancy Catherine 71
Wilson, Nancy J. 22
Wilson, Parlena 61
Wilson, Peggy A. 39
Wilson, Polly 23
Wilson, Rebecca 15
Wilson, Rhoda 17
Wilson, Sallie A. 51
Wilson, Sally 64

Wilson, Sarah 6
Wilson, Sarah G. 40
Wilson, Sarelda 46
Wilson, Surilda 40
Wilson, Susan 63
Wilson, Tempy J. 1
Wish, Levesta 43
Witt, Marth 59
Witt, Mary E. 15
Woard, Levina 38
Wood, Judia 34
Wood, Lizzie 35
Wood, Mary Jane 38
Woodard, Louisa 56
Wooddard, M. J. 50
Woods, Ailsy 59
Woods, Feroby 21
Woods, Margarett 13
Woods, Martha 8
Woods, Mary 38
Woods, Polly 59
Woods, Polly Ann 52
Woods, Sarah 43
Woods, Sarah C. 49
Woods, Timanda Magusta 53
Woodson, Eliz. 14
Woodson, Jane S. 61
Woodson, Julia 41
Woodson, Martha M. 37
Woodson, Obedience 44
Woodson, Sarah 20
Woodson, Sarah 48
Woolem, Armelda 73
Woolen, Herriet 73
Woosley, Sarah 1
Word, Mary J. 34
Word, Rachal 11
Worley, H. J. 41
Wright, Cenia 1
Wright, Elizabeth 51
Wright, Hester A. 56
Wright, Mary 14
Wright, S. 27
Wright, Sally 4
Wright, Susan 56

Wright, Susanah 27
Wyrick, Angeline 41
Yancy, Elizabeth 6
York, Catharine 12
York, China 73
York, Jane 67
York, Nancy 12
York, Patty 12
York, Polly 73
York, Tissie 57
Young, Eliza 6
Young, Jane 53
Young, Martha J. 45
Young, Nancy 49
Young, Syrena S. 11
Young, Vicey 44
Yount, Amanda E. 71
Yount, Anna 39
Yount, Manda 44
Yount, Mary 8
Yourk, Amanda 73
Zackary, Mary Ann 15

www.ingramcontent.com/pod-product-compliance
Lightning Source LLC
Chambersburg PA
CBHW052117090426
42741CB00009B/1847